Snatched From The

Snatched From The Flames

Anita Hydes

with

Michael Tony Ralls

New Wine Press

I dedicate this book to my mother who despite all her own struggles, was always there when I needed her.

Anita Hydes

New Wine Press
P.O. Box 17,
Chichester PO20 6RY

British Library CIP data

Hydes, Anita
Snatched from the flames
1. Converts
I. Title II. Ralls, Michael Tony
248.2′46 BV4916

ISBN 0 947852 07 7

Typeset by Input Typesetting Ltd, London
Printed in Great Britain by Hazell, Watson & Viney Ltd, Member of the BPCC Group, Aylesbury, Bucks

Contents

Introduction

It has been my privilege to know Anita for many years. I have known her as a drug addict, and as a born-again Christian serving others in need. One has only to meet her to know that Jesus is still in the business of miracles.

The title for this book came from some Bible verses in Jude (v 20–23). These words perfectly describe Anita's life. As the story progressed, we were both very aware that certain episodes were not only painful to write about, but could also bring us under the accusation of sensationalism. But we felt it important to include these elements for two reasons. Firstly, to offer hope to anyone who is trapped in the same dark tunnel, and secondly to highlight just what is happening to problem people in society today. The welfare state has no permanent solutions to offer. Doctors cannot cure drug addiction. Prisons do not reform characters. Only Jesus can provide the answers to life's pain and difficulty. We believe that it is time the Church stopped debating social issues, and made Jesus known instead.

With over a hundred thousand children in care, overcrowded prisons and mental hospitals, a terrifying increase in drug addiction, and one in ten children being abused sexually within their families, we believe that this book has a very relevant message, and we pray that its two goals will be achieved.

Michael Tony Ralls
December 1984

Prologue: Dead to the old life

As I walked inside the chapel with my friends, I realised that the building was packed. My heart beat faster as I looked at the sea of faces, but gradually I began to pick out faces that I knew, people who I knew cared for me; people who had been praying for me. I began to feel calmer.

I was taken to a side room with the elders. When we went out again into the chapel the people were already singing. Somehow I seemed very much on my own, and yet I felt the peace and comfort of Jesus with me. It was only four months since I had taken the decision to become a Christian, and at that time I didn't fully realise the significance of the commitment I had made. I was thirty-one years old and behind me were seventeen years of misery and squalor: years of drug addiction, prison, lesbianism, prostitution. Yet here I was, sitting in this chapel, waiting to be baptised.

The service seemed to flash past. We sang; an elder preached about baptism and what it symbolised; then at last it was time for my baptism. I walked forward to give my brief testimony. I was nervous and conscious of my inadequacy to express what I really felt. I needed help to get down the steps to the pool: my body was stiff and uncoordinated – another side effect of years of drug abuse.

It seemed as though I was under the water for a

long long time. Somehow I felt that I was at rest, and as I was lifted up from the water I heard the sound of singing. They were singing the chorus that I had chosen: the one with the line 'I would rather be a doorkeeper in the house of the Lord than to take my fate upon myself'. It was beautiful to come out of the waters to hear those words sung, for they meant so much to me.

As I moved unsteadily up the steps of the pool I experienced a tremendous feeling of peace, acceptance and cleanness. I knew that I had honoured God and because of this I felt He had drawn very close to me. It was good to have been able to do something for Jesus – He had done so much for me. He had died for me and given me this brand new life, and now I had had this opportunity of standing up and testifying to all that He had done for me.

After the service, as I sat alone at home, I could only say to the Lord, 'Thank you, Jesus, I love you.' I was on my own but yet not alone. I knew that at last I had a future and a life that was worth living.

1: Damaged Roots

I was born in the East End of London. My father had spent many years at sea with the Merchant Navy. I didn't know much about his roots except that he came from Cuba, had ten brothers and had spent a lot of time living in seamen's missions and hostels around the world before eventually settling in London where he was later to meet my mother.

My mother had been born and bred in the East End of London. From what I gather she had had quite a rough childhood. She had got married very young and I feel that this was the cause of many of the problems that were to surround me and affect me as a child.

We lived in a small room in a large apartment house in Bow, though my memories of it are indistinct. My earliest memories are of my father kicking my pregnant mother down the stairs, and the atmosphere of tension and violence which pervaded the place every time Father was at home. We all lived in one room which did not help, of course. Often my father would go away for weekends with other women. When he came back he always seemed to be aggressive and I was soon to get used to this atmosphere of fear, tension and violence.

I remember my mother hiding food away because Father would turn up, eat all the food and disappear again, leaving us with nothing.

Most of my memories of this early period of my life, particularly up to the age of eight years old, are very disjointed. One incident that stands out in my mind however was the day when, at about four or five years old, I had gone out to the outside toilet. My mother had often warned me to stay away from an old man who lived downstairs. He was known as Uncle Tom. I never really understood why we were warned to stay away from him. That day, when I came out of the toilet I was in my nightdress and it was dark. Uncle Tom appeared, picked me up and took me down into the cellar. He laid me on a table, and even though I didn't understand what was happening I suddenly felt very frightened. He switched on the light over my head and then I heard my mother's voice calling out for me. The old man lifted me off the table and took me upstairs, warning me not to say anything to my mother. Even though nothing actually happened, I still remember the fear I felt.

I remember that I often, for one reason or another, stayed with my grandmother, who lived in another part of the East End. I have fond memories of these visits. It was good to get away from that one room in Bow. I really enjoyed staying with my grandmother, but unfortunately I would always have to go home again.

When I was eight, two things happened that were to affect me deeply. First my grandmother died, and then we moved to a flat in Wapping, a riverside part of the East End. It was good to be in a place where we had more space to move around. We had a three-bedroomed flat but unfortunately it was situated in an area which was reserved for problem families.

The block of flats itself was situated on the wharf overlooking the River Thames. The crime rate for the area was exceedingly high and it was not unusual to hear of nearby rapes or robberies. We were also very aware of the many men in the area who were in the habit of exposing themselves. It seemed almost natural that the children living here, in this block of flats, would be caught up in a similar sort of lifestyle. Fear, suspicion and tension became part of everyday life. Family life was no better. I always seemed to be being beaten, and I came to accept this as normal. But I really missed being able to go to my grandmother, and even at that age I felt very trapped.

Sometimes as a result of these beatings I couldn't go to school because of the bruises that covered my body, and my only escape from the violence at home would be across the road with a friend of mine whose mother would make me welcome in her house.

There are two incidents from that period which stand out vividly in my mind. At about ten I, along with my brothers, was hanging around a pub called the Prospect of Whitby. Many rich and famous people used to come there and children used to hang around outside offering to look after their cars while they were inside the pub. Sometimes we would get half a crown for doing this. One day a car drew up and I ran towards it, wanting to be the first there. However, instead of somebody getting out, I was grabbed and pulled into the car and driven away. I was very frightened as I looked at the driver – a man aged about thirty. My brothers chased after the car but soon had to give up. The man drove me off to a dark place and there interfered with me sexually. I just didn't know what to do about this. I felt I couldn't say anything to my parents as they would be angry with me for being outside the pub in the first place. I felt so alone. I had been violated and yet there was nothing I could do about it.

The second incident happened when I was about fourteen years old. I hadn't gone to school for some reason and when I came home my parents knew about it. I had asked a friend to come home with me as I was frightened of my father's reaction. However, this did not protect me. Dad grabbed my arm and in front of my friend pulled me violently into the bathroom which was downstairs. He threw me into the corner and then started to kick me. He was wearing hobnail boots and it seemed that there was no area of my body which he did not kick. I cried out to him to stop but he seemed to have gone crazy. He then took off his thick leather belt and started hitting me and swearing at me at the same time. By now my friend had run out crying. She went looking for help while my mother tried to drag Dad off. I managed to crawl out of the bathroom while she distracted his attention, and ran on into the bedroom.

Even though I was used to receiving severe beatings both from my mother and father, this was the worst one that I had ever had. That night I cried myself to sleep. I was aching all over. I felt so trapped and unable to do anything; I was totally at the mercy of the whims of my parents.

When I awoke the next morning my dad had gone to work. I dragged myself out of bed. I found I could hardly move as my body was still aching all over. My mother, too, had gone out and I was on my own in the flat. I heard a tap at the door and the caretaker's wife who lived opposite us was standing on the doorstep.

'Are you all right?' she asked me. She must have heard my screaming the night before and guessed what had gone on. 'Do you want me to get the children's officer down?' she asked. I just shut the door in her face and started crying.

My thoughts were in a state of confusion. Certainly I was frightened and angry but yet I didn't want my parents to get into trouble. Also I was worried about what would happen if I was taken away from them, and even at that age I thought 'better the devil I know than the devil I don't know'.

I just cried and cried. I felt no one could help – I was isolated and alone. There was a social worker attached to our family and yet whenever she came to our house it seemed that my mother would demand all the attention. Even at that age I could understand in some ways why she behaved like this. She had not had an easy time with my father, and she had had three children before she was twenty-one. Yes, I could understand my mother's needs but nevertheless, this didn't help me with my own problems.

I did have one friend, and in the beginning I had been able to seek refuge at her house. However, it wasn't long before even this haven was denied me. My mother used to come over, make a big scene and then drag me off home. Because of this my friend's parents eventually refused to allow me in.

Now I no longer had a hiding place to go to, I was stuck. In the end my friend introduced me to 'Chutlers'. This was an all-night cafe where the local pimps, prostitutes, drug-addicts and villains would gather. The advantage for me was that it was open twenty-four hours a day and therefore I always had somewhere to run to if things got too bad at home. The disadvantage was that it was to bring me into contact with a side of life which was nearly to lead to my destruction.

2: The trap is set

I was about fifteen when I first started going to Chutlers. As I got older the occasions when I ran away from home became increasingly frequent. My parents would always report me for this and at first, when the police picked me up, I would be taken to the police station. I usually wasn't kept there for more than a few hours and then I would be sent home. It was never long before things were back to normal, and after being beaten again I would run away. I seemed to be caught in a circle of going home, being beaten, running away from home to get away from the beatings and being picked up by the police and returned home. This vicious circle carried on for quite a while until one time, after being picked up by the police, I was sent to the local remand home for care and protection.

The remand home was to be my first taste of what it was like to be in an institution. It was a large building and the first thing I was conscious of was the lack of privacy, and a different sort of tension and fear which seemed to rule the place.

It appeared as though the system was there to degrade us. I remember the shame of having to have a strip bath and the impersonal way that the doctor looked me over for the medical examination. I found the whole process both dehumanising and embarrassing. However, I was soon to get used to the routine of stripping, being examined, having a bath and having my clothes taken away from me.

The uniform of the remand home was made up of a dress which was green with white spots on, black shoes, thick tights and plain underwear. No make-up was allowed. We slept in large dormitories and I can still remember the nights, lying awake, listening to the groans and shrieks coming from the girls who were asleep around me. I used to feel so frightened, vulnerable and frustrated with the deal that life had handed me.

I had several spells in that remand home and was soon accustomed to its daily routine. Most of the day was spent scrubbing the landings and cleaning, and I quickly adapted to this way of life.

The circle of running away from home and being put into the remand home was soon to be broken. I was arrested as a person who was in need of care and protection. What this really meant was that I was becoming a nuisance to people. I can never quite understand what happened after that, as I was then sentenced to approved school for running away from home. It seemed to me that this would not help a lot. There was so much violence at home that I had to run away, and I had not actually committed a criminal offence. It seemed yet again that I was being punished when I had done nothing wrong.

However, I was quite glad not to be going back to the remand home as I had had my first fight there; a black girl whom I had nothing against had wanted to stir up trouble as I had inherited some of my father's colouring and looked slightly foreign. I was soon to learn the lesson that even if one was fright ened inside, one had to fight back and appear as vicious as possible in order to survive.

I was never naturally violent, and yet, because of

the life I was living, I became increasingly aggressive. Later, even when the police were arresting me I would start to fight back, and I found myself becoming instinctively pugnacious and gradually found myself in more and more fights.

I have only vague memories of approved school, as I didn't stay there very long. It had a homely sort of atmosphere, very different from the remand home, but I soon absconded. In fact I left the first day I arrived there. After climbing out of a window and thumbing a lift I was soon back in London.

I was to escape from this approved school many times. When on the run I didn't even have my parents' home to go to. This meant that I went without sleep and food often for days on end. I would go at night to places like Chutlers, as this was the only place which was open, and I would just sit there. I learnt just how little food and sleep one can manage to survive on. Sometimes, when desperate, I would steal milk or bread from outside cafe doorways. Now and then some of the prostitutes who knew me and felt sorry for me would put me up or buy me a meal. It was during this time that two significant things happened to me.

One night, when I was at Chutlers, I noticed a girl taking some pills from her handbag and swallowing them. She looked up and saw me looking at her. She then dipped her hand into her handbag.

'Take a couple of these, dear,' she said, offering me some pills. I took them and swallowed them down with a drink of coke. They didn't taste very nice but I will never forget the effect that they had on me at first. First of all there was a tingling excitement inside me as the drugs began to take their effect in my body. Next came a feeling of confidence and, whereas I was naturally shy, I was suddenly able to talk and chatter to anyone about anything. Then came the surge of energy where I was able to talk and dance all the night through. The pangs of hunger temporarily disappeared as well. Later there was the comedown which was to lead me to take other drugs in order to combat it. I was to learn that these drugs had originally been known as 'purple hearts'. They were amphetamines and acted as a stimulant.

Nowadays as I read the papers and see TV programmes about young people who are caught up in drugs, my heart goes out to them. I am sure that many of them are like I was. They come to a crisis in their lives, and they are offered drugs as a way out. At first it seems to be an easy escape, but they cannot see the future and the penalty that they will pay for taking this apparently easy option in the face of life's difficulties.

The second significant thing happened when I had run away from approved school another time. Despite the fact that I had mixed with a lot of different people involved with prostitution, I was myself still a virgin. In some ways I was proud of this, for I knew so many girls who had lost their virginity and had been involved in all sorts of sexual relationships, and yet here I was, still a virgin, despite all the things that had been going on around me.

On this day, I was lured into a man's house – I was still pretty gullible in those days. I was beaten, almost strangled and raped. As I stumbled away from the house I felt filthy and violated. It seemed that the whole world was against me, but I couldn't complain because I was on the run. I walked around all that night; I felt so alone; there was no one I could turn to. I cried and cried, but this was the last time I was to shed tears for a long time because

I believe that night I reached a state of ultimate disillusionment with the world, and in a way I grew up.

The strangle marks on my neck and the bruises on my body took a long time to fade away, but it took much longer for the inner bruises to fade. In fact they have only just recently begun to be healed.

Almost as a direct result of this attack, I became a lesbian. I developed a sexual fear of men because of this incident and this was compounded by the fact that my mother had told me terrible things about what would happen if I slept with a man. She warned me that I would become pregnant and told me that sex was painful. I had seen the violence between my mother and father and this, coupled with all the other experiences, affected me drastically.

I not only became a lesbian myself, but became actively involved over the years in leading other women into this way of life. I have become very aware, since becoming a Christian, that so many people are affected by the things that happen to them early in life. I'm sure that many, like myself, have had experiences which have influenced their attitudes and damaged them emotionally. I know it is important to teach people to know Jesus as a person, but I feel it is just as vital that deliverance and healing should be part of the general ministry of the church.

By now I had very quickly graduated from 'blues' or 'purple hearts' to methedrine, which was a much stronger stimulant. This came in glass ampoules and at first I used to swallow the methedrine, which was a liquid, with a drink of coke. One day I was persuaded to inject it, and so had my first 'fix'.

As I look back I am amazed at the short time that

passed between my taking those first pills which were to help me to stay awake at night, and having my first fix. I was even more amazed at the rapidity with which I was to become a fully-fledged drug addict and the changes that had happened within me as a person over the last twelve months. I was cynical, violent, hardened and only sixteen years old.

3: Hooked

It seemed that only bad things had been happening to me and there were no influences for good in my life. At that time I don't think I'd come across any real Christians, although a friend of my mother's was a Jehovah's Witness and to my understanding in those days that was the same as being a Christian.

This woman had known my mother for many years and even now is still constantly trying to convert her to the JWs. She had several children and Janet, her oldest daughter, was just a couple of years younger than me so, as they lived upstairs when we were living in Wapping, I saw quite a lot of them. I did agree to go to a few meetings with them, but this was only because they asked me and because they were the only people I really knew.

I don't remember much about the meetings except that there was a man standing in the front preaching, who seemed to run it all himself. I believe there was some singing and I generally felt lost in the midst of all that was going on. However, I felt there was a general warmth in a lot of the people and I can understand how many people are attracted to cults such as the JWs.

I never really got enthusiastic about it and was put off further one day when my mother's friend was talking to her and she said something about her son being damned because he had left the JWs. Also I noticed that when people were coming out after worshipping they all started gossiping. Mind you, this is something I have come across quite often in Christian circles as well!

Despite the lack of religious influences, I often cried out to God, particularly when I was being beaten a lot. I would often cry to God, asking Him why I should have parents like this when other people's parents seemed to be so different. I was very bitter about the life I was leading and certainly blamed God, yet somehow even though I cried out to Him, I never seemed to get any sort of answers or comfort.

I am sure that there are many who are crying out to God today, who need to meet with people who can direct them to Jesus.

I had also come into touch with what I now know to be the occult, although I never saw it that way at the time. Through my mother and brothers I often had my tarot cards read and I distinctly remember a day when the death card came up for me. I also went to see a woman called Dolly Crutch who was a clairvoyant with a crystal ball. I didn't get much comfort from any of the things she said and a friend of hers said I would be dead by the time I was twenty-five years old.

I didn't really want to get involved in such things, but because of the family pressure I just went along with it, although I was a bit frightened. I didn't really understand the evil of it all, but I certainly didn't want to go any deeper.

I have no recollection of meeting clergy or Christians during all this period of my life, and I can't say what my response would have been if I had. In my remand home and approved school experience I don't remember coming across any chaplains. So all in all there were only negative spiritual influences in my life at this stage, though at the time I had no understanding of what was happening. All I realised was that I had no control over circumstances, and seemed to be just being swept along by a strong current which was certainly hurting me, and which was eventually to lead me to hurt other people.

It was quite surprising the number of times I had been allowed to go back to the approved school. I can't remember exactly how often I ran away but it must have been half a dozen times or more. I was never away for more than a few days and yet so much seemed to happen during those times.

I think one of the main reasons I was given so many chances was that people were sympathetic towards me. I was still young, and many knew of the circumstances which had led me to the sort of trouble I was in. However, even their patience was to run out.

From the time of my taking that first fix, the drug side of my life had escalated. I soon discovered that it was most convenient to get myself registered with what was known then as a 'bent doctor', who was willing to give you a prescription for a certain amount of money. Also at that time there were a lot of drugs around: heroin, cocaine, and all sorts of other drugs, mainly prescribed through these doctors. Much of the time I felt I was on top of the world. I was getting enough drugs to satisfy my own needs and also enough to sell to others so that I could eat, hang around the clubs, and have enough money to spend.

However, I also knew that the time would come when I would be picked up again and returned to approved school. I found myself involved in situations which I never thought I would be involved in. It is very surprising how much can happen in one's life in so short a time. Now and then I resorted to prostitution when I needed some extra money. Because I was so young I tended to hang around with women who were older than me.

I still had some contacts with my family, although this was mainly through my brother Paul who would occasionally come and look for me. I had found that my relationship with my mother and father had totally broken down and I never saw them.

It was through Paul that I was eventually to be arrested and sent to Holloway prison. One day, when I was yet again on the run from approved school, I had been sitting with an older woman in a pub. My brother had come in and tried to talk to me. He was very concerned for me and I must have looked in a bad state for he tried to drag me out of the pub. He was in a very emotional state himself, crying and shouting at the same time. He was asking me why I was hanging around with prostitutes and what on earth was wrong with me. I tried to run away from him up some stairs. I knew that he was just trying to get me away from that place, but I also knew that he was aware of what had been happening at home and felt some sort of concern for me.

However, somehow I just panicked and yelled out and started to fight and scream and kick. Paul also panicked. Unfortunately, a police car came by at that moment and Paul, because he was obviously well out of his depth, called to them and asked them to come in. They arrested me, and also the friend I had been sitting with. This really was the last straw.

I didn't want to be arrested again, because by now every time I was arrested I was starting to feel the effect of drug withdrawal despite the short period that I had been addicted. In the end I started to attack the police and they found it very hard to subdue me and get me into the police car. I fought them all the way back to the station. Because I was high on methedrine I seemed to have abnormal strength. Looking back on it I must have behaved like an animal, but one doesn't think like that at the time. I remember, as I drove away, seeing my brother in tears. He had tried to help but somehow it had all gone wrong.

When we reached the station I was taken in and taken to a room where a policewoman came and searched me. I still had to be restrained even then, but I was certainly used to the routine of being searched and stripped.

They found seven heroin pillls on me and, after I had been charged, I soon found myself on my own again in the cell. I sat there looking at my surroundings: the usual hard boards with just a pile of dubious looking blankets on them.

My mind was still spinning from the drugs I had taken earlier that evening, and I spent half the night thinking about all the things that had been happening to me. I really resented being locked up in this cell.

They pulled me out of the cell later to ask me a few questions concerning the drugs that had been found on me, and after this I was yet again returned to the cell where I stayed up all night, unable to sleep. In the morning, after being given breakfast and a chance to wash my face, I was put into a police van and driven off to the Magistrates Court.

As I sat in that van I felt exhausted. By now the

effects of the methedrine were beginning to wear off and I was coming down. There were windows in the van so one was able to catch a glimpse of the outside world. All the way on the short journey to the court, I was looking out of the windows at a London which seemed so alive at this time of the morning, and yet I was not part of it. The previous night had been like a dream, and even though I was very much part of what was happening I was somehow looking in upon myself and seeing myself doing all the things that I had done that night. I was kicking myself for being so stupid about the heroin, which I could have got rid of quite easily, but I seemed destined to get myself into trouble.

For some reason I thought that I would get away with this offence, and was quite confident of being allowed free from the court. I was still in a daze when I was put in the cells under the court, and the time soon came for my friend and I to be taken up. There we were in open court, facing the magistrates.

It was always a surprise to me to see the number of people to be found in a Magistrates Court and, still in a dopey state, I just gazed around at the faces of the different people. Eventually I started to listen, and I realised that I had been remanded to Holloway prison for forensic reports concerning the drugs that had been found on me. There had also been some mention made of a social enquiry report concerning my home circumstances and background. A policeman had stood up and objected to bail so I was to be taken back down to the cells. I was still barely aware of what was happening around me. However, it did register that I would not be free that day, but that I would be staying that night, and the next six or seven nights, in a place which was well known to me by repute: Holloway prison.

4: Holloway and Borstal

I had heard a lot about Holloway from some of the women I had met in the cells beneath the court. Other people I had known at Chutlers and other places had also spent time there, usually short sentences for common prostitution, so I had some idea of what it would be like. I had already built up a fear of the place.

It was a lovely sunny day. Again I looked out of the window of the police van, noticing people bustling to and fro, all going about their daily business, while I looked at them like an observer from another world. I was feeling a complex mixture of emotions – resentment at what had happened in the pub, fear of what was going to happen at Holloway, and a frustration at the vicious circle of my life which, rather than getting better, seemed to be getting worse and worse.

Soon the van drew into a large, dark, old, grey granite building. We drove up to the gates which opened up like a monster ready to swallow the van that drove through. They shut with a resounding crash behind us. There was a feeling of finality about it.

Once in the reception, I was subjected to the inevitable strip, bath and search. On coming out of the bath I was made to spin around while I was inspected for things which I might have tried to smuggle in. I still could not get used to this ultimate humiliation of being naked in front of a stranger, and being looked at in such an impersonal way.

I then saw the doctor who asked questions and, finding out that I had been arrested for heroin, gave me a couple of physeptone pills which were to help me with my withdrawals. He also told me that I would be put into the hospital.

After the bath we had been given a bundle of clothes. They were typical institutional uniform: a green dress with white spots on, a grey skirt, a green blouse which was for best, thick tights, plain underwear and flat shoes. We were also given towels, sheets, knives and forks, and we were taken on to the different parts of the prison where we were to remain for the next few days.

I was soon in the dormitory where I was to remain for the next few weeks. Everyone looked up at me as I walked in and I felt very self-conscious. A girl indicated an empty bed and, feeling very nervous, I went straight to it and put my stuff down. It was not long before I was surrounded by girls. I noticed that many of them looked rather butch (that is, they were women who assumed the male role in a lesbian relationship). They often dressed and had their hair cut in a way which made them look more manly. I realised that most of the girls in the dormitory were lesbian.

They were mainly after the cigarettes that I had brought in with me, and I found it good to be able to talk. The usual questions were asked: 'What are you in for?', 'How long have you got?'

Most of them had been involved with drugs and we were soon talking about the people we knew and the different experiences that we had had. After a while a nurse came along with the medicine trolley and we were all given our medicine in little plastic containers which we drained to the last drop. I then lay on my bed and tried to get to sleep.

I soon settled into the routine of the hospital and I found that time passed quickly. Our medicine was brought round regularly during the day. We could play music on the record player, but many of the songs reminded me painfully of various aspects of my life out there in the world.

I went through the inevitable interviews, as I had to have reports concerning my living circumstances, so that the probation officer and the social services could put in some sort of report with a recommendation to the court.

The remand period passed and it was time to go to court. It was good to get out; at least it meant a trip away in the van, and away from the routine of Holloway. At that time I was still assuming that I would get away with the offence and that I would be free that evening.

I looked with eagerness again out of the little window where I could see the world, but all too soon we were at the court. Here I was again in the cells under the court, waiting to go up.

When I came up before the magistrate, I began to realise that things were not going quite the way that I had expected they would go. The magistrates said that they didn't want to deal with my case and I was remanded to the quarter sessions which, in those days, were held at the Elephant and Castle. I was taken down again to the cells under the court and then returned to Holloway to await the quarter sessions.

By now I was beginning to worry, as I realised that by going to quarter sessions I was more likely to receive a sentence. This time, after being taken through the reception routine, I was taken in another direction with the majority of those who had come in with me that day. After going through many gates we came to a door and there I was for the first time in the main wing of Holloway prison.

It looked huge and ominous. There seemed to be rows and rows of cells and different landings and everything was very dimly lit. Because it was evening by the time we got there, there were no people on the wings or the landings except for a couple of officers in the centre. We stood there huddled in a bunch, holding our clothes and blankets, waiting to be allocated to our cells.

The building echoed with bangs, bells, shrieks and the sound of trays hitting doors as people tried to get the attention of the duty officers. After a while I heard my name called and an officer indicated that I should follow her. I was taken up to the second landing, where I was locked into a cell by myself.

The cell was as austere as usual: the small bed with a pile of blankets, the chamber pot, the furniture and then, worst of all, as I looked up – the bars on the window.

I dropped all that I had been carrying on the floor by my feet and suddenly panic overcame me. I hadn't had my medicine. I rang the bell, kicked the door and screamed until an officer came round. I explained to her that I needed my medicine and she said she would go and get a nurse to bring it round. It seemed a terribly long time before the nurse eventually came and gave me some medicine. I then made up my bed and lay down, staring at the ceiling.

I must have drifted off to sleep, for the next thing I remembered was the bell ringing. It seemed to be so early. I staggered out of bed and onto the landing.

Already there were small queues of women and girls waiting to empty their chamber pots in the urinal. The smell was terrible.

That night I had felt I would not be able to cope, but somehow one does. I was soon settled into the routine of getting up in the morning, going down to get breakfast, eating it, and then going on to sit in the shop all day packing spoons. The weeks soon passed and I was taken back to court. I still hoped to get off. However, when I was taken up before the judge I began to realise that this time I would go down.

I heard the sentence passed – I was to go to Borstal. Somehow it was a relief as, although I knew that I would have to go back to Holloway for a time, at least this would mean that I would soon be out of Holloway into a different environment. I wasn't quite sure what Borstal would be like, but somehow I knew it would be better than Holloway.

I was sent back to Holloway to wait until I was allocated to a Borstal. Because I had run away from the approved school so much, I knew that I would be put into a closed Borstal.

I soon heard that I was to be sent to Bullwood Hall Borstal. It was with great relief that I packed all my gear and went down to reception, where I was given my own clothes for the short journey to the Borstal.

I don't remember a lot about Borstal. I have the impression of a large house, set in beautiful grounds. The building had cells in it rather like a small prison. The uniform and the routines were very similar to those of Holloway, although the uniforms did change halfway through my time there.

Most of the girls at the institution were involved in lesbianism but though I was emotionally a lesbian, I was not then very active in any way. Here lesbian activities seemed to be happening all around me, but somehow I kept myself to myself. I often wondered why the officers didn't stop it but somehow they seemed to accept it as part of life. Now and then someone would get caught in the act and get put on report.

Again, as I look back over my life, I begin to realise how many Satanic influences there are in such places. Many there were regularly playing around with ouija boards and some were actively involved in séances. Sometimes these were a bit of a laugh, but at other times people really seemed to be getting through to something. I was still frightened of this sort of thing, and somehow seemed to resist getting involved in anything of that kind.

However, in Borstal, an experience happened to me which I can still remember vividly to this day, even though it was so many years ago. I had had an ordinary day, just going through the routine of doing my work, eating and doing the usual things that one does to get through a sentence. My cell had been locked up and the lights had just gone out. Suddenly I felt a presence of evil in the cell. It was as though my body was frozen and powerless. I even tried to call out to God, and yet somehow the very words were frozen in my mouth.

It is very difficult to explain what happened that night, but as it was something which happened again later on it is important to go into the details of this first experience.

It seemed as though something was overpowering me, a weight trying to smother me. I think, as I look back, I can see that it was the devil trying to take possession of me. This 'something' seemed to be getting closer and closer. I felt as though it was trying to get inside me and yet physically I was unable to do anything. Mentally, however, I still tried to resist.

At last it passed, and suddenly it seemed that the presence had left my cell. I leapt up and started shouting for an officer. As she came I prepared myself to tell her about my experience, but then I stopped. It would have seemed so stupid, and what could I tell her anyway? So when she looked through the peep-hole and asked me what the matter was I just said that it didn't matter, and she left.

I didn't have a clue as to what had happened as I was in a daze. It was only when I became a Christian that I really fully understood what had happened that night. I realised that the devil was trying to possess me and that, in fact, something was given over to him that night.

I have only recently been set free from the fear that followed on from this incident. I think it is important to realise the satanic influence that is prevalent in our prisons, and when you seek to reach out in Christ's name to people you have to acknowledge that the devil is often the person you are dealing with. He is the one who has possession of so many people's lives.

Apart from this incident, Borstal seemed to pass uneventfully. I kept myself to myself and just coasted through trying to keep out of trouble. It was soon time for me to be released into the world again.

I went back into the world looking for those things that I had become used to before coming to Borstal. Drugs seemed to be the main object of my life. There seemed to be nothing else, outside of that, worth living for.

5: 'Mass murderers'

It was really great to be out of Borstal. For weeks I had been building up in my mind what it would be like when I got out. I returned to my parents' home although things were still very unsatisfactory there. By now I was eighteen years old so there was no more physical violence. However, I was not made to feel at home; there were constant bickerings and tensions and I felt that I was not really wanted there.

Because of the situation at home I soon moved out into a room in Cavel Street which is just off Commercial Road in the East End. It was one of those small bedsits in a large apartment building, and my room was at the top of the stairs.

Chutlers was no longer the centre of my life. In fact I hardly ever went there. However, through a girl whom I had met there, I started to get introduced into some of the West End clubs. I began to go down to these clubs regularly and was rapidly back into the swing of night life and drugs. I soon forgot that I had been inside.

There were a few complications in my life. Even though I was still able to get drugs quite easily there were no longer many bent doctors around. Several doctors had been arrested for illegally prescribing drugs, so this meant that there was a limited supply of drugs around. The only place I could get registered as a drug addict was at a clinic which had been set up by the government, and the only drugs we could receive there were physeptone or methadone, as it is commonly known, which was synthetic heroin. Synthetic heroin had been brought over to this country by two doctors who, I believe, were genuinely trying to do something about the massive heroin problem. Unfortunately methadone turned out to be just as harmful and addictive as heroin, but this was only discovered later. Because I had been in prison I was only allowed three amps a day which, of course, was very little to me. However it was better than nothing, and in time I would be able to build up the prescription, as I took more and more drugs.

Going to the West End brought me into contact with a wider circle of people. Most of the clubs I went to were all-night clubs; there I met the people who lived on the streets, and there were a lot of them around in those days. Many would come in to sit in the club all night as they had nowhere else to go, and then would go off into the city until they turned up the next night. It was in one of these clubs in the West End that I first met Tony, a person who was later to have a great influence in my life, but at the time was just another lonely individual. We used just to meet and sit and talk and generally hang around together during the night. In the morning we would go our own ways. He was like many at that time, and in fact many young people today are still living the same sort of life. He was also involved with drugs and seemed to have no point or purpose in his life. Like many who hung around those clubs, he had done some time in prisons and Borstals.

It is funny the sort of relationships that one can

form in those circles. Tony and I met regularly, but there was nothing emotional or physical in our relationship.

It was a few months later that I first encountered Viv. Like myself, she came from a very violent background although I did not know much about it. I had heard from others that she had been very badly beaten by her parents and as a young girl had started going into the clubs. Although she had never taken heroin she was, however, taking pills which were mainly stimulants.

Gradually, through other girls in the clubs, we got to know each other and it wasn't long before Viv moved in to live with me at my room in Cavel Street.

It is important here to emphasise a couple of points. Many can only think of lesbianism in a sensational way. I think it is important to underline the fact that Viv and myself were drawn together by a common need for love and security, for which both of us were desperate. Our interdependence and desire for love did eventually lead us to a sexual involvement, but this was the direct result of our emotional needs.

In our society today there are many young people getting caught up in homosexuality and permissiveness in different ways, and I am sure it is because they are looking for acceptance and love. Like myself in those days, they do not realise the difficulties and implications of what they're getting involved in.

I was also still seeing Tony. In fact Viv by now was going out earning her living as a prostitute, and Tony and I would sit together waiting for her to come back after going with a client.

It seemed quite normal for Viv to do this kind of thing, as most people around us were into some sort of way of earning a living which was not quite normal. Many were involved in satisfying the whims of the so-called 'straight society' to earn enough money to support their own lifestyles.

For a few months Tony, Viv and myself met quite regularly at night. Tony would go his own way in the morning while Viv and myself would go back to our room in Cavel Street.

Tony was soon to return to prison, and I was the indirect cause of this. We were hanging around Piccadilly one night. I had just come out of hospital after an overdose and was feeling very shaky. A man approached me asking me if I would go with him for money. I swore at him and told him to go away. However, he was not put off and he grabbed hold of me and pushed me down some stairs. I screamed and Tony came running over, grabbed hold of the man by the hair and kicked him in the face. The man scuffled off, I met up with Viv and went on home. However, I heard later that Tony had been arrested for assault on this man. The man had apparently been working in the police canteen and he had brought the police back the next morning. He had identified Tony, and as a result of this Tony received six months imprisonment.

Viv and I had by now moved into a small flat in Mile End Road, in another part of the East End. The flat was upstairs over a launderette facing onto the main road.

We were getting closer and closer in our relationship as in many ways Viv was the first real friend that I had ever had. She continued to go down to the West End regularly and I myself was taking more and more drugs. One day I was introduced to a Chinese man, who was to become my regular connection for Chinese heroin, and he asked me if I would supply for him.

This was to change our lifestyle considerably. Viv was able to stop the prostitution and I was able to keep her, which I felt was important. The dealer would give me approximately two ounces of Chinese heroin a week and I would sell it and make enough money to live on and also have enough drugs for myself. Even though by now I was receiving six amps of physeptone a day from the clinic, this was having no effect on me because by now I was accustomed to using heroin, which was much stronger.

There were two of us in our building pushing drugs, myself and Pauline, a lesbian who lived downstairs and whom I had known for many years – in fact we had gone to school together. Because we realised that we were under constant surveillance from the police and got raided every few days, I would hide my drugs in a drainpipe out in the street.

Here I was at twenty-one, one of those people whom everyone likes to hate – the pusher. But most people don't realise that being a pusher is very much part of being a drug addict. One has to sell so that one can buy and, as the habit increases, so one has to make more and more money to support it. It was inevitable that because of all the police surveillance, I would eventually get arrested, but somehow we just lived from day by day.

That period of my life seemed at the time to be a very good one. I had a friend in Viv; we had somewhere to live; I was needed; I had enough drugs and money to live on. All the things which I felt at the time were necessary for fulfilment and happiness were around me. However, this was not to last long.

About one year after I first started to be involved

with Chinese heroin, I was arrested. It was just an ordinary day. I had needed to get some money together so that I could buy some heroin. To do this I would have to go down to the West End which I knew was a bit risky, but I needed the money quickly, so that I could buy some more heroin from my source.

I caught a taxi to Gerard Street and it wasn't long before someone approached me, wanting to buy some drugs. I stood in a shop doorway and got a small packet of heroin from my trouser pocket and was ready to pass it on to him when suddenly I saw a policeman's helmet appearing from the back of a lorry. The buyer seemed to disappear from the scene very quickly so I realised that I had been set up. Apparently the police had been watching us for quite a while, and later on I found that not only had they arrested me, but also most of the other members of the Chinese heroin gang including many of the top people. This meant that I was up not only for the offence of pushing drugs, or having drugs in my possession, but I was also up on a conspiracy charge, which I knew was very serious.

I was taken to the police station, searched, cautioned and then released on bail. Even though being arrested was a bit of a shock, somehow I had always known that I could not continue pushing Chinese heroin and get away with it for ever.

On being released I went back to our flat. The police had organised a big drugs operation throughout the whole country, although of course I didn't know about it then. This was to lead to a shortage of drugs on the street. Within a few days of my arrest I went back down to the West End again to buy some drugs. I was desperate, as recently I had always had enough drugs, and suddenly I had none.

As on the previous occasion, I had taken a cab to Gerard Street, except that this time I was desperate to buy instead of to sell. I waited for many hours with the man who had come along with me. He had helped me to sell in the past, so I trusted him. After a couple of hours he managed to get some drugs for me. I had allowed him to do this as I was too weak to go searching around to see who had any drugs around Gerard Street. I needed a fix so desperately. Eventually he bought the drugs for me and kept them in his hand while we walked quickly down the road and I hailed a taxi. Just as I was about to enter the cab he passed the drugs into my hand. I wanted to get away quickly, not only because I didn't want to be arrested, but also because I was desperate to have a fix. Immediately the drugs were in my hands I got into the cab, shut the door and breathed a sigh of relief. It wasn't long before the cab had to stop at some traffic lights a few yards down the road. Two men suddenly appeared at the door, opened it, got in, and held me back against the seat, laughing at me. I think I had been set up yet again. They directed the taxi driver to take us to Vine Street police station. There again I was charged, but of course this time I knew I was not going to get bail.

I was soon back into the old familiar routine, appearing at the magistrates court, being remanded in custody and being sent back to Holloway. This constant remanding and going back and forth to court went on for several weeks. The case was to hit the headlines as, all in all, there were nineteen of us involved.

Viv used to come in and see me, and somehow I could see that she was already beginning to crack up because I wasn't around. Eventually we all received bail. We had all been remanded to appear at the Old Bailey, and so I went back to stay with Viv to await the court case. Things were very hard for me then, as I no longer had an easy supply of drugs. Another complication had arisen, as immediately I had gone into prison, Viv had started on drugs. I thought the best thing I could do for her was to get her registered so that at least she would be able to get some drugs from the clinic.

Tony had briefly re-entered my life. The last time I had seen him was when he had attacked the man who had approached me for prostitution. He then turned up briefly after leaving a Christian rehabilitation centre he had gone to. Since then I had discovered that he had become a Christian, but was very much torn between his desire to go on as a Christian and his need to go back onto drugs. He had disappeared out of my life again at that time. Suddenly he had turned up and had started to visit Viv and me, and had brought along with him a friend who was training to be a solicitor. By now Tony was solid in his Christian commitment and definitely didn't seem interested in drugs any more. His friend Graham was going to prove to be a very useful friend as it was he who was eventually to find me the barrister who would represent me at the Old Bailey.

As I look back I try to remember possible times of spiritual significance. The sense of an evil presence smothering me that I had experienced in Borstal had repeated itself many times while I was living with Viv. Each time I had cried out to God but it never seemed to help. It seemed that if there was a God He didn't seem able or willing to do anything about my situation although, as I look back, I can see that God was indeed at work bringing different individuals into my life at different stages.

Over a year was to pass between receiving bail and appearing at the Old Bailey. This period is rather a blur for me, but I have vague recollections of trying to buy drugs, take drugs, read depositions and hearing about different people who were informing on each other.

Now that my Chinese heroin supply had dried up I had to live on what I was getting from the clinic, but thankfully another source did turn up for me. I was still able to go to Harley Street where there remained some doctors who were willing to give out prescriptions for a price. It seems there was always a source of supply. Once one had dried up another would open.

At last the time for the court case came. It was to last approximately ten weeks, but I had pleaded guilty after the first week and was put into Holloway to await sentencing. I went in worried about Viv and with the knowledge that I would be lucky if I got seven years, as this was what my barrister had told me.

The day I was to be sentenced arrived, and I was surprised to be given only a two and a half year sentence. Despite the degradation to which I had been brought, I was still somehow able to respond to what the judge said to me as he sentenced me. He called us a herd of mass murderers, and these words really struck home. I felt guilty and condemned, and yet there didn't seem to be anything that I could do about it.

6: Living with death

Even though I was very relieved to receive two and a half years, rather than the seven years which I had expected, once it sunk in I realised that two and a half years was quite a long time. It was the longest sentence that I had ever received. And I was to spend most of it in Holloway prison.

I was beginning to be sick of drugs and sick of the whole scene and would have welcomed the opportunity of being able to get my life together in some way, and yet it seemed that in Holloway all the pressures were against this happening.

I had Viv on the outside, and I worried about her constantly. I didn't receive any visits from her, but she would send someone else from the scene to come and see me occasionally. She used to write to me, and I realised that she was going deeper and deeper into drugs, as she seemed to have nothing left now that I was in prison.

On the inside there was constant pressure, and I often wondered what it must be like for young girls who have had no experience of imprisonment suddenly to find themselves in the situation that I was in. I had other institutions behind me, and had at least some idea of what it was like to be inside, but even then I was not prepared for the pressures that were to surround me in Holloway.

The court case had been well publicised, so most

people knew what I was in for. This, of course, did not help as it was impossible not to become the centre of many people's attention. I didn't particularly want any sort of relationship with any of the women that were in there. However, in the end I realised that I would have to become close to someone in a lesbian relationship; it was expected of me and pretty well impossible to avoid.

Drugs were also very hard to avoid. At that time it was quite easy to obtain physeptone, heroin and most other drugs in prison. So I continued with my drug habit while in Holloway, despite the fact that I might possibly have wanted to use this period of life to get away from drugs.

I think people should be aware of the massive drugs problem that we have in Britain, not only in ordinary society but also in our prisons. I know that my friend Tony had his first smoke of dope when he was in Exeter prison.

I had been through Holloway before of course, but I'd never actually served a long sentence there and I certainly found that it was very different from being in for an occasional remand.

The smothering incidents continued to happen. In fact they seemed to occur more often now. I still called out to God but it still didn't seem to help. I think I felt I was getting weaker and weaker and less and less able to resist these attacks. Again, I can clearly remember that it seemed as though something, or rather someone, was trying to get inside me and to take over. I seemed powerless to be able to do anything about this and didn't really understand what was happening. Of course I fully understand now.

There are many people who do not believe in Jesus nowadays, but even more who do not believe in a personal Satan. I certainly believe that there is a devil and I know that he is a person possessed of much power.

While I was in Holloway my sister Maria was stabbed and her lung was punctured. I felt so powerless to help her, in my situation. One of the worst things about prison is that one does feel so powerless to intervene in anything that is happening outside. I did go to church a few times then, and I called out to God for help, yet again it seemed I was always shouting out to Him and yet nothing seemed to be happening. In the end, rather than shouting out to Him, I think I was shouting *at* Him.

All my bitterness and frustration seemed to pour out at times like this and I felt so impotent and unable to understand what on earth was happening in my life.

One could write a whole book about experiences in prison, and yet it is not easy to describe what prison actually does to you. It is difficult to put into words. I got through the routine and survived, like many do in prison, and yet I think I was marked by the experience, particularly in my emotions.

Time passed and at last I was ready to be released. I had been sent to an open women's prison to do the last few months of my sentence, but unfortunately I had lost some remission. There was an officer there who seemed to be sexually interested in me and in the end, because I rejected her friendship and was fed up with her advances, I lost my temper with her one day and was put on report for this.

The injustice of the situation got to me as I stood before the governor's desk. I flew into a rage and ended up assaulting the governor and fighting with the other officers. Realising they were too many for me, I fought my way out of the office and ran off upstairs to my dormitory, but a couple of the officers followed and caught up with me. Because I had been hurt in the scuffle I was said to have been 'wounded in action', and because of this I did not lose very much remission. I was returned to Holloway and the date soon came up for my release.

Despite the way I had been thinking at the beginning of my sentence, after all that had happened in Holloway, particularly with the availability of drugs and the pressure for me to be actively involved in lesbianism, it seemed hopeless to try to get away from the sort of life that I had become used to. It was almost automatic for me to go back to drugs and to all that I had known before I went in.

Viv had by now been registered as a drug addict for quite a while. She had really gone downhill in her health. It seemed that she, like so many others I had known on the scene, had no resistance to the drugs and the lifestyle that went with it. A lot of friends whom I had known when I was first on drugs had died by now and I could see that Viv was getting weaker and weaker and seemed to be always ill. We could never now recapture the time of happiness that we had once had.

Viv had arranged a week's supply of drugs for me for when I got out, so it was straight back into the old routine. It wasn't long before I was able to get registered again at St Clement's drug clinic, and was getting my regular supply of amps each day. It seemed inevitable that this would happen as it did not seem possible for me ever to live any other sort of life. By now I was a few years into the drug scene and there didn't seem to be anything else in life.

Two or three years passed. Here and there I would hear of yet more people dying. I think thousands upon thousands of young people have died in the Western nations from overdoses of drugs. I know that I saw virtually all the old friends who had started out on drugs with me die. Even Pauline, the lesbian girl who had lived downstairs, was now dead.

My own health was deteriorating rapidly. I had been getting convulsions for a great many years now, but had never known what they were. Eventually I had a scan and found that I was, in fact, an epileptic. I was told that the condition was incurable and was given Epanutin, which was supposed to help me. I took some of them from time to time, but they made me so sick that in the end I didn't even bother taking them. Of course, these convulsions were among the usual side-effects of drug-addiction. I also had abscesses and sores and was getting physically weaker and weaker.

I had been worried about Viv for quite a while as her body just didn't seem to be able to cope with the drugs. Her health seemed to be deteriorating very quickly, and eventually she had to be taken into hospital.

She was only going in for an abscess as far as I knew. I didn't think much about it, as this was very much part of being a drug addict. Because I thought it was something relatively trivial, I didn't even bother to go in and see her for a week. This wasn't because I wasn't concerned; it was just that I was in a bit of a mess myself. I was taking a lot of different drugs by then and I had to wheel and deal all the time just to get what I needed. I just didn't seem to be able to find the time to go and see Viv.

When I eventually did get round to seeing her, I was shocked by the way she looked. She was barely conscious, although I sensed that she knew that I was there. The nurses had told me that she hadn't been eating and asked if I would encourage her to eat. I knew that she was more ill than I had originally thought she had been, but it still didn't get through to me how dangerously ill she was.

One day, on visiting her, I found that Viv seemed to be much better. I even thought that this was the turning-point, she was on the mend and would soon be coming home. She had spoken to me and said my name for the first time in days, so I went home quite relieved that she seemed to be recovering.

I was to be woken at 5.30 the following morning. The police had come and asked me to go to the hospital to Viv. They told me that she had taken a turn for the worse, so I got myself together and they took me up to the hospital. I appreciated the fact that they seemed to be very sympathetic and genuinely concerned.

I had always been the strong person in our relationship and had always looked after Viv. I felt that somehow I would be able to impart strength to her and that if I encouraged her then she would come through this time.

On going into the room I found that she was semiconscious. She was immediately aware of me, for she tried to struggle up when I came into the room. I started chatting to her and generally trying to encourage her, thinking that if I could get her to fight a bit then she would come through. As she was in a feverish state, I was constantly mopping her forehead, and at the same time inwardly I was crying out to God. I felt that I wanted to see Viv either come through this alive or die quickly and peacefully. When I look back on all these different situations in which I cried out to God, I realise that if anyone had challenged me at that time I would have said that I didn't believe in Him, and yet my instinctive reaction when I was desperate was always to cry out to Him in some way.

The end was to come quickly. At about 9.00a.m. Viv suddenly had a convulsion, and within minutes she was dead.

Viv's death affected me more than anything else that had happened to me up to that time. A lot of friends had died, but I had never seen them die, and Viv was in many ways the closest friend I had ever had. I wasn't a Christian then and yet I remember thinking how empty she looked in death. It seemed as though her body was now just a shell, and that Viv had gone on somewhere else.

I had done all my crying before I had got to the hospital, so I had no tears left to cry. I was relieved in many ways as I knew that Viv would not be suffering any more pain. She had had such a short and painful life. She had suffered so much over those last few years and, like many I had known, she had never seemed to have a real chance in life.

I was on my own now and yet I didn't think too much about it at that time. I left the hospital and went back to the flat. I had enough drugs with me, so I didn't have to go out and buy any. Somehow I was just numb – unable to think or feel any more.

have said that [illegible] he was ill, and [illegible] I was [illegible]
always [illegible] but to [illegible] so away.
The [illegible] about [illegible] and [illegible]
she was dead.
[illegible] had [illegible] covered [illegible] the [illegible] I was [illegible] looked [illegible]
[illegible] the [illegible] as I [illegible] had [illegible]
[illegible] that night I [illegible]

7: Hospital

I missed Viv a lot but, as people say, time is a great healer and also my life was centred on the problem of how I was to get enough drugs to keep me going.

I was still registered as a drug addict at St Clement's clinic, although I only received six amps of physeptone a day from them. This was not enough to sustain me as, like many registered addicts, I had become used to getting other drugs to supplement those I got from the clinic. My source of heroin had dried up but another source of supply, as always, was on hand. This was the Harley Street doctors and other private G.P.s who were willing, for a price, to give out prescriptions to addicts. There was also still a certain amount of drugs around on the streets which were obtained either through addicts who were getting bigger prescriptions than they needed, or those who had broken into chemists or got drugs through other means.

God didn't figure anywhere in my life at this time. I had prayed when I had been with Viv and yet, as usual, it seemed to me that there was no answer.

I was still living at the same flat and stayed there for a few months after Viv's death. I continued to go up to Piccadilly and it was while going up there on one of my regular trips that I came across a girl called Maria. At that time she was getting hundreds of amps of physeptone from various doctors. We began to share them, and I would help her with selling them. So in many ways life was back to normal and I had another source of drugs.

It seemed likely that in the end I would die of an overdose or some drug-related disease and at that time I just didn't think there was any other way out. In fact, on reflection, I don't think I even thought about wanting a way out. This had become my normal life and would continue until I died, probably as Viv had. I was physically very weak by now, from the side-effects of several years of drug abuse.

For some years I had been noticing a woman who was often to be seen around Piccadilly, particularly on Sunday nights, giving out sandwiches and soup and talking to the addicts. At first I didn't know who she was, but later I discovered that her name was Joan Askew and that she was a Christian. She seemed to be respected by all the people she spoke to, and she was also trusted, which is unusual in those circles. I have known her to take people who had overdosed to hospital, and do many other kind actions, which may have passed unnoticed by the rest of society or even by the church, but was very much appreciated by the people whom she was seeking to help.

Joan always had a cheery smile and would often say hello to me and we would have a short talk, of no great substance really except that she would always show concern as to how I was. I was quite happy with this, as I didn't want to know anything about Christ at this time and would probably have rejected Him if Joan had sought to share the gospel with me.

One day I found out that Joan knew Tony, who

had left London to get off drugs, and now and then she would pass on a message from him or just send his regards. One day she asked me for my address. It is interesting to note the way that links are forged in a person's life. Starting with my links with Tony and with Joan, I can see how, at different stages in my life, I was brought into contact with the people whom I needed at the time. Once this had meant that I got a good barrister to represent me in a court case, and this time it meant that I had someone here on my own scene who was in contact with the Christian world outside.

I suppose this is what the Body of Christ is all about – individual Christians linking together and working as one. Later, when I heard that expression, I realised that I had seen the Body of Christ at work at grass roots level, and I certainly knew what it meant.

I had long since left the flat which I had had with Viv and had been living in a squat in Poplar, still in the East End of London. I then moved on from this flat and had been staying at various addresses, usually only for a short time. My lifestyle continued very much the same as it had always been. Maria, with whom I was hanging around, was gradually getting more and more involved in bouncing cheques. I myself did not take much of an active part in this but I did start to be involved with disposing of the goods that had been obtained through this means.

I still had some minimal contact with my parents although as always it was never very good. I used to go back and see them occasionally but I sensed that they were very ashamed of me, and because of this I never stayed long.

On the other hand, my sister Maria still wanted to know me and was always glad to see me. She cared about me, perhaps because I was her bigger sister, I don't know, but I know there was love there. However, she was also morbidly obsessed with thoughts about my death and was collecting photographs, as though she assumed that I would be dead soon. There was certainly justification for her belief at that time.

The smothering experiences which I had first had in Borstal recurred through the years and were still happening. They came every few months or so, and every time it happened I felt I was getting physically weaker and less and less able to resist.

All through the years I had been 'fixing', or injecting myself, in various places. Most of the veins in my body had collapsed and, because I was fixing barbiturates, I was always having abscesses.

One day my legs started to swell up. At first I carried on as normal but soon it spread to the bottom half of my body and I was bent right over so that I could hardly walk. I was in a state of constant dull pain but somehow managed to stagger on with my routine for a couple of days. One day I woke up in the morning and just about managed to get enough strength to get up, grab a cab and go to the chemist and get back and take my drugs. At that time I was staying with two girls – prostitutes – who were also on drugs. Even though I was very ill I still had enough sense to take the drugs quickly, as I realised that those girls would have stolen them if I had not been careful.

I was unconscious most of that day, and every now and then I would wake up and beg the girls for some water, but they would just ignore me as I had not given them any drugs. This carried on for about a week. I would get enough strength up to get to the chemist and come back, and then I would just lie on the bed all day. The girls didn't like this much and made it very obvious. They were certainly not going to do anything to help me. I was dirty, had lost a lot of weight and was hardly able to do anything for myself.

A woman of about forty who was a lesbian and an alcoholic had popped in a week or so previously, and she turned up again one day and found me lying on the bed. I think she must have realised what was going on and she lost her temper and started shouting at the girls. As a result of this they got me off the bed and cleaned me up while this woman went and phoned for an ambulance.

I was taken to the London Hospital. I don't remember much about it, but from what I can gather I had definitely got septicaemia. I know they were also worried about a lump in my stomach, but because I refused to allow them to do an internal examination they were not able to pursue this much further. Besides this, there was also a clot in my groin, so I was altogether in a real mess.

I didn't know it at the time, but the hospital had informed my parents that there was not much chance of me coming through. I suppose even if I had known it wouldn't have made a lot of difference, as this was the normal end for people who were on drugs.

I had never really had a fear of death, although I don't think I was particularly thinking about dying at the time. Sometimes now people ask me what was going on in my head at that time and to be honest, I must admit that hardly anything was. I was just existing and this was part of the lifestyle I was involved in – one became ill from time to time.

Something very important happened while I was in the hospital. When Joan Askew had taken my address she had passed it on to Tony who was living in Devon and, as a result of this, Tony had written to me. The address I had given had been my sister Maria's and she had sent the letter on to me in hospital. It was nice to hear from Tony and I was glad that he was off the drugs scene and OK. He certainly seemed happy enough in his new life. He had married and by now had one child and there was another on the way. In the letter he offered to put me up, and suggested that if I ever wanted to get away from the drug scene I would be welcome to come and stay with him. It was good to hear from him, but I was not very interested in leaving London.

He had mentioned something about Christianity and, in fact, had finished the letter with 'Yours in Christ,' but at that time it just didn't mean a thing to me.

I was in hospital approximately a month and in the end I discharged myself because I was so fed up with lying around in bed and having needles stuck in me. By now I was feeling much healthier and, to be honest, I just wanted to get out and get on with my own life.

8: A way out of the trap

On leaving the hospital I went home to my parents. Obviously it was not the place I would have chosen to go, but the fact was that I was in a very weak state still, and needed to be looked after. I could hardly walk but I was still receiving my prescription from the St Clement's drug unit and I now had to limit myself to taking nothing but my prescription for a time. I just didn't have the strength to go out looking for drugs.

Staying with my parents was very difficult. I felt there was some genuine love and concern in their hearts for me and yet in another way I felt they were very ashamed of the way I looked and in some ways resented my presence. I never quite knew where I stood with them. But I was aware that I didn't have much choice, as I was so weak and ill at the time, and I knew that if I went off on my own I would certainly not last long.

After a while I suddenly decided that I might as well go down to Devon for at least a week or so, just to get away from London for a break. There wasn't a lot I could do in the city anyway, in the condition I was in, and living at home wasn't exactly a happy experience. I rang Tony and asked if it would be OK to come down. He seemed to be delighted that I would be coming, and we soon fixed a date.

It was good to meet up with Tony again. He picked

me up from the station, as they were living in the heart of the country. The house that they had was a little bit run down. It had about an acre of ground and was a mile from the nearest village. There couldn't have been a greater difference from the East End of London.

Tony had changed a lot. Obviously he was older, as a few years had passed since I had last seen him, and he seemed a lot more quiet and content. It was good also to meet his wife and their daughter.

However, it was all a bit odd to me. Before we would have our meals he would say grace, which I found a little bit embarrassing. We went out for a few walks here and there although of course I couldn't walk very far and I knew he was definitely trying to share something with me, but to be honest I just couldn't understand and wasn't really interested.

I can't remember much about that week as at the time I wasn't feeling well and I was still taking my drugs. I went to one or two meetings and I also met some of Tony's Christian friends, but basically I just remember being in the country for a week. It soon passed by and it was time to go back to London. It had been good to see Tony and his family, and he emphasised before I went back that if I ever wanted to come away from London totally, there would always be a place in his home.

At the time I didn't really expect that I would ever take him up on that offer, although it was good to know that there was someone somewhere who would be willing to have me at any time.

On returning to London I began to go through a time of total disillusionment with the scene I had known for so many years. Perhaps this was linked to the fact that many people were praying for me. I know Tony and his family had been praying for me for many years. Also I knew Joan and other Christians had been praying for me. I am sure that the prayers of Christians influence the minds and hearts of people.

I was by now in my late twenties. I was terribly weak physically and I no longer had the energy or the enthusiasm to dash around as I used to. Wheeling and dealing was out for me now, and because of this I started to take fewer drugs. I was starting to keep to my prescription only which was very unusual for me.

I was now utterly sick of the lifestyle which had killed Viv, Pauline and so many others that I had known, and had wrecked my own health. Yet I was unable to think of any other way of living – I was trapped. I think the only way I can describe this period of my life is to compare it with the way a spider wraps up a fly. The fly is alive and yet it's as good as dead, because the spider is just waiting to devour it. I felt at that time as though I was totally wrapped up in a lifestyle which was killing me, and yet there was nothing I could do about it. There were no laughs left. All the kicks and thrills had gone and life was just a dull monotony of pain, both emotional and physical.

I continued to live at home, although the tensions were still the same. I was living there out of sheer necessity, but it did bring me into closer contact with my parents. Occasionally I would still go down to Piccadilly. Here I would bump into Joan Askew who continued to be friendly. Even though I didn't particularly want to know about Jesus or the gospel, one thing I did realise was that someone cared. Christians need to realise that, as they show care and love to others in this world, it can often be the first step towards a person knowing the Lord.

It was on one of these occasions in Piccadilly that I was arrested again. The charge was attempting to supply, yet all I had on me was the physeptone amps for which I was registered. Two policemen had accused me of trying to sell some of them. I was a little bit worried about this as, with the two and a-half year sentence for supplying on my record, besides other drug offences, I felt I could go down for a long time. I was taken to the police station and remanded on bail awaiting Knightsbridge Crown Court.

Joan had kept in contact with me and one day rang me up and suggested it might be a good idea if I took up the offer that Tony had made, and went to Devon.

I had lived in the East End all my life and couldn't imagine living outside of London. The only times I had been out were to go to Borstal or approved school, apart from the short holiday that I had had with Tony and his family. Although I kept pushing the idea away from me, it kept coming back. Again, I believe people were praying for me at this time. It seemed that there was nothing left in London for me anyway. There was certainly no future where I was, and I had the court case coming up. Instead of my health improving I was getting worse and I seemed unable to get myself together. I had had to go into hospital again for an operation on my leg as I had an ingrowing abscess and hepatitis. It certainly seemed as though my body was giving out. It was a combination of all these things which in the end led to my decision to go to Devon.

I went to my clinic and told them that I wanted to go to Devon to get away from the London scene, and asked if they could arrange for my prescription to be transferred to a local surgery in Devon. They were dumbfounded that I would even think of leaving London. My mother, however, was very encouraging and Joan was, of course, delighted. I am sure many people's prayers were answered that day although I would not have put my decision down to prayer at the time. On talking to Tony and people like Rita Nightingale I have learned that they were released from the circumstances that they were in because people had prayed for them, and I continue always to encourage people to pray for those who are trapped, in whatever way it may be.

In the end it was all arranged. The date of my departure was coming up, and I must admit I had some second thoughts. I think possibly the only reason I went in the end was because my prescription had been transferred through to Devon, so I would have to go there to pick up my drugs.

The actual day arrived. I got up in the morning feeling that I was near enough going to my death. To go to Devon seemed to me like going to the farthest ends of the earth. Certainly it was all right for a holiday, but actually to live there became more and more inconceivable. In my mind I had formed an escape plan of only staying there for a few weeks.

I slung a few clothes into a carrier bag and then my mother came out with me and we walked along towards the tube station. I don't think either of us said a word between getting on the tube at Whitechapel and arriving at Paddington station. My mother started crying, and there were tears in my eyes, although I didn't openly cry, as this was something which would have been unthinkable in those days.

My mother was there supporting me. As I look

back at my life and my parents there are so many apparent contradictions. Yes, I did have a bad childhood and yes, I didn't get on very well with my parents, and yet Mother was always there. Whatever the reason, she was always there at the court cases and here she was supporting me as I sought to make this effort to get away from the drug scene in London. As I look back in perspective through those years I realise that my mother had her own problems and they were very serious ones. It is so good that the love of God has helped me to be able to understand this. I can now see with more clarity the amount of support she did in fact give me, and perhaps this was the only way that she could show her love.

The train journey was terrible in some ways. I felt like jumping off at every station where the train stopped. Certainly I had known Tony well in the past, but this was a different person I was going to, almost a total stranger. He and his wife were nice people, but still strangers, totally unrelated to the world from which I was coming. I also recognised that all their friends would be from an alien world. I had tremendous surges of emotions – a mixture of fear and trepidation. I felt very vulnerable and scared, but somehow I managed to stay on that train.

Later, I read in the Bible about the Israelites leaving Egypt and I suppose in some ways that was rather like me. I was still on drugs and yet I was leaving the whole culture in which I had been enslaved for so many years. I felt naked, vulnerable and exposed. I was already missing the protection of the world that I was used to. All I had left from that world was six amps of physeptone which I would be able to pick up from the local chemist. I think that if I hadn't had this I would never have made that trip. Here I was at thirty years old starting a brand new life, and yet in some ways I was caught between two worlds; I had nothing to go back to, I wasn't sure of what lay ahead, and yet I wanted to live.

9: In the country

Even though I had begun to lead a brand new life in Devon, I still had a routine that was based around drugs. I had to go to the chemist every day to pick them up. At first I went to Cullompton, and Tony used to give me a lift there every day in his car. This was a twelve mile round trip through country lanes – so very different from the East End. Surprisingly enough I didn't miss London as much as I had expected.

There was another man staying with Tony and Linda. He was a Scot, and known as Jock. He had been an alcoholic for many years and had been staying with Tony and Linda for the last two or three years, so was very much part of the home by the time I got there. He was a Christian and he seemed friendly enough, but later complications set in. Unfortunately he decided he had fallen in love with me, and I found it very hard to know how to react.

I knew that Tony and Linda really felt that Jock should be moving on by now, as he had been with them so long. He had a daughter in care and Tony, at the time, was trying to arrange it so that his daughter could come and stay with him, with the ultimate aim of them having their own place.

Simon was another lad who came to stay at the home quite soon after my arrival. Of course I knew that Tony and Linda had had many people living with them before moving to this place, and there always seemed to be people coming for help. It seemed to me that many of them were actually exploiting Tony and Linda, despite the fact that several of them were professing to be Christians. Simon particularly stands out in my mind, as he had come from a Youth Custody Centre to which Tony used to go quite regularly. In front of Tony, Simon was a radiant Christian, always saying 'Praise the Lord!' and yet, immediately Tony and Linda were not around, he would talk to me about the village girls he was having sex with, swear and almost laugh at Christianity. Like many young lads he seemed always to be trying to impress, and he particularly wanted to impress me for some reason.

Simon didn't stay long. As soon as he got a job he moved on to other accommodation so that he could do the things he wanted. It seemed to me that he had just used this family and home for his own purposes.

I knew that Tony's attitude was that everyone deserved a chance and it was very much up to them what they did with it. I was to encounter many people like Simon and I think it was good for me to come across such people. I somehow knew that if I myself ever did consider making a commitment to Christ, I would either mean it truly and sincerely or not do it at all.

I soon learnt that Tony and Linda were just ordinary people. They certainly loved God in their own way and sought to serve Him and to be Christians, but living with a family one can see the pressures and tensions that can come into a home. There were bad times of quarrels and rows and yet in a way this was encouraging, to see that this was real life and that God deals with real people in real situations.

I found the children very demanding. They always seemed to be noisy and wanting attention, but of course this was my first prolonged contact with children in my whole life, so I had many lessons to learn about myself.

I met many of Tony and Linda's friends and I particularly remember one man, Commander Metters, a grand old man of eighty, well over six feet tall. I remember him coming into the room one day and just gently kneeling down by the couch where I was sitting and talking to me. I knew this man was very rich, and he was obviously very old, and yet here he was wanting to communicate and share and I felt very much at peace in his company. Another important thing I noticed about him was that he seemed fully to understand the problems of young people today, despite the fact that he was so old. Through this dear old man I was to come into contact with Phil and Jenny.

Phil had moved into the area a few weeks earlier with his wife Jenny and their three children. They had rented a house from Commander Metters, and after Commander Metters had talked to Phil about Christ, he had suggested that he should go up and see Tony. On the first evening that Phil went to see Tony he had prayed for the baptism in the Holy Spirit.

Phil was an interesting character. He had been a scientist and, through his experiments, had come to realise that there was a God and had then issued a challenge to God. He had said, 'Right God, if you are there, the doors of Liverpool Cathedral will be open for me to get in.' When he went to the Cathedral the doors were chained up, but he could open them just enough to squeeze in, and because of this he committed his life to Jesus. It always amazes me the different ways that people come to know God. Phil's experience, like that of any person who becomes a Christian, was unique, and yet somehow in this strange way he met with Jesus.

I met Jenny, his wife, later on. She wasn't a Christian at that time but she was a lovely, compassionate sort of person. So now they were close neighbours, by country standards anyway, as they only lived three-quarters of a mile down the road.

The first few months passed surprisingly quickly. Tony had got a job in a meat factory and I had managed to have my drugs transferred from the chemist to the local village health centre which was only a mile down the road. This meant of course that I was able to go and pick up the drugs every morning.

It wasn't long before Jock moved on. A place had been found for him and his little girl. I was very relieved to see him go as it was a constant worry and embarrassment for me, knowing how he felt about me. This meant for a short while that I was to be on my own with Tony, Linda and the children. I was certainly conscious that I was in a Christian home as grace would still be said at the meal table and Tony, despite the fact that he was not going to church at this time, still did a lot of Christian work in various prisons and Youth Custody centres around the country. Also various Christian friends would pop over to see Tony and Linda, so I was constantly in contact with people who were Christians. I can't honestly say what was happening in my mind at that time as I seemed to have constructed so many barriers around me.

Tony had not been going to church for quite a

while before I came. I discovered that he had only been to church for some five years over the previous ten or so years. Here and there he had had some bad experiences with various churches which had put him off, but this was something that I was only to discover later. I knew he was constantly emphasising the need for a personal relationship with Jesus first, rather than getting into any sort of denominational mould, although I didn't understand what this meant at the time.

The time did come however, when Tony, Linda and the children started to go to a church in a local town. It was known as a community church and sometimes I would go with them. Jenny and Phil also started to come along with us. I was not expected to go to this church but I was quite glad to get out of the house for a bit. I was surprised at first, for this seemed to be a very open sort of church. It was held in a school assembly hall and the services seemed to go on for a long time, although I would go out for a cigarette every so often. People seemed to dance around a lot and the music was quite good. There were lots of choruses and the people taking part in the services certainly seemed to be enjoying themselves and very emotionally involved in what was going on.

In a sense it was quite easy for me to be there as it was such a large gathering of people. I was able just to sit there and not feel any personal pressure upon me. I could see that most of the people seemed to be having a good time, but somehow the personal message wasn't coming through to me. Everything was happening around me and I was just an observer.

Life continued with this routine of going to the chemist, going out shopping with Linda and the children, and not doing much else really except sitting around and reading comics. The smothering experiences which had been part of my life for so long still continued to happen, often when I was on my own in my room. I talked to Tony and Linda about them but all they could do at the time was to offer to pray for me. They tried to explain to me that it was probably a demon or Satan attacking me, and that some sort of deliverance or spiritual help was needed, but I always rejected their offer of prayer – mainly, I think through embarrassment. When one has led the sort of life that I had led, and has built a protective wall around oneself for many years, it takes a long time before one can start to open up even about one small area of one's life. I was certainly not ready then to open up about anything. Later I discovered that there were times when Tony was getting very frustrated, but he always bit his lip and didn't try to put any pressure on me spiritually. I know that this was right, as at that time I would have not responded and, if the pressure had been too great, I would probably have walked out and gone back to London.

One day Tony told me that John, a friend of his from the past, was coming to stay with them. I wasn't sure what to think about this, as I had already had the experience of Simon and Jock living in the home. Still, I thought, it was their home and in some ways it would be quite nice to talk to someone else, particularly as John was just off the drug scene.

John was a sixteen stone Londoner who had become a Christian about ten years before at the same time as Tony. They had both made a commitment in the same drug rehabilitation centre, where they had shared a room. Since then John had gone back to the drug scene and had done a couple more prison sentences. His marriage had broken down and he had remarried and now had three children.

Because of the drugs John had ended up in a mental hospital, and his second wife, Barbara and his children had left him and gone to live in a children's home in London. Tony had left a message for John, rather in the same way as he had done for me, to say that if he ever wanted to get away and start again then there would be an opportunity for him, so John rang up one day and asked Tony if he could come and stay.

I quite liked John. He was a barrel of laughs – a typical Londoner with a real Cockney sense of humour. He had had a very rough past. He had been born in Holloway prison and had apparently been taught to steal at his mother's knee. I could certainly identify with him in many respects, and it was good to have an ex-Londoner around.

It wasn't long, however, before I saw that he too was just out for himself. He wanted his wife and children back, and it seemed to me that the only way that he could achieve this was by staying with people like Tony and Linda. As I got to know him better and better I realised that he had exploited many people through the years, and I felt that he was yet again using people, and particularly this home, as an opportunity to get his wife and children back. It wasn't long before Tony took John up to London to visit his wife and children, and as, a result of this visit, Barbara said that she would come back to him. Tony later went up to London again with John to pick up Barbara and the three children, who were all boys under six years old at the time. It was good to meet Barbara. She, too, was someone who had suffered a lot in her life. She had been in trouble with the police in the past, and had certainly not had an easy life with John. There was now absolute chaos in the house. What with Tony's children and John's children, and two families living together, as well as me, we found we were getting under each others feet all the time.

It seemed to me that John started to change very quickly. Perhaps this was because he had achieved what he wanted; his wife and children were now back with him. Again I was to come across this hypocrisy of someone acting in one way in front of Tony and Linda, and in a different way to me and his family. I sometimes thought Tony was a bit soft, as it seemed to me that he was allowing himself to be used all the time, but again his message always came through, that everyone deserves a chance in life and it was up to them what they did with it.

Because of the chaos in the house and the need to have a change of surroundings, I used to pop down to see Jenny and Phil. It was nice to speak to other people and I got on well with them. One day Jenny told me that she had become a Christian. I could certainly see the difference in her, even physically. She seemed to be radiant and very much alive in a new way. Her conversion had happened at a crusade which was run by an evangelist called Don Double. There had been a great deal of activity surrounding this crusade as, of course, a lot of organisation was needed to launch it. The crusade had taken place in a tent in a large town about seven miles away. All the churches in the area had publicised the crusade and were involved in taking people to it. Linda had gone on several nights and one night Tony took me too.

Even though I didn't admit it at the time I had

very mixed reactions, both to Don Double and to the crusade. He was a big man, and his manner sometimes instilled fear into me, and yet something stirred up inside me that night. Something definitely did get through. I never took any action at the time, but when I look back on it I realise that the Holy Spirit touched me that night. On the way to the crusade I had been frightened and certainly didn't feel I belonged there. On the way back I was very quiet, but I soon dismissed from my mind all the mixed emotions that I had experienced.

Since Jenny had become a Christian the next step for her was to be baptised. It was going to be a double baptism, as Linda had never been baptised as a believer by total immersion. The baptisms were to take place in the local river. Tony had asked people to come and help and they included members of many different churches in the area.

It was an unusual day because it had started out being very windy and overcast and yet, as we went down towards the river, suddenly the sun came out and it was a beautiful evening. The setting for the baptism was very picturesque: to the right was a stone bridge, and the river stretched down along the fields. I stood on the bank as I watched Linda and Jenny walk out into the river. A man called Keith, who was a social worker, had been leading the service with Tony's support. There had been some chorus singing and Keith had shared what the purpose of baptism was, and explained what was going on. There were some young lads leaning over the bridge watching all that was happening. I wondered what was going on in their minds as they looked down to see these two mature women allowing themselves to be ducked in water.

One thing I do remember from that day was the

radiance of both Linda and Jenny, both of whom were dressed in white. I suppose looking at it from a non-Christian viewpoint it was absolutely crazy for two grown women, who were both mothers, to allow this to happen to them, and yet somehow I realised that this was something very special and it meant a lot to them.

I was coming towards the end of my stay with Tony and Linda. A lot of pressure had been building up. John had really started to play around now and a couple of times Tony had caught him using the phone without paying. One day a major conflict arose when John called Linda a snob and said that she couldn't understand or relate to people like him. This hurt me a lot as I knew that Linda was a loving and caring person who always had an open home for people in need.

In the end Tony and Linda had decided to move on and to try to find somewhere else to live, and to let John and Barbara and their children have the house. I thought this was crazy. It seemed to me that John was winning on all sides and that Tony was just backing away from the situation. However, I did realise that they just couldn't carry on living together and Tony seemed to think that he could easily find somewhere else. Even before I became a Christian I witnessed miracles happening. In this country area most housing was either occupied by locals who had been there for years, or bought up by people for holiday accommodation. Tony and Linda prayed for a house and, even though everyone told them that it would be impossible, they managed to find a little cottage within three or four miles. It was at a reasonable rent which they could afford.

Because of them moving on I had been offered the opportunity of going to stay with Jenny and Phil.

Obviously I was very grateful for this offer and decided to take them up on it although, as always, I was apprehensive about the move as I didn't like change. However, after a while I found I had nothing to worry about and I soon settled in with them and was very glad that they had offered me a home.

10: Trouble again

I had been in Devon for just over a year by now. I was certainly learning to lead a new lifestyle, which was totally different to the one I had previously known. Many things were getting sorted out in my life, particularly in the practical realm. In some ways, perhaps, looking at my life, one would think that little had changed, but it was in fact a great advance for me to have become used to living with and relating to families with children, putting up with the pressures and problems, and still being able to keep to my six amps of physeptone a day.

There were still certain court cases that had to be cleared up. I had been to Knightsbridge Crown Court where I had received a conditional discharge, despite the fact that I had been found guilty of attempting to supply drugs. I had been very worried about this case as, with my two and a half year Holloway sentence behind me, I thought there was a possibility that I could be put inside again. However, Tony had driven me up to London and spoken up in court for me and I was very grateful for his presence. At other times in the past I had been very much on my own but now there were people alongside me. My mother, as always, had also turned up yet again an indication of her care.

However, there was another charge which worried me a lot more. Maria, the girl with whom I used to knock about in London, had been arrested. Others were pulled in with her in connection with bouncing cheques, and somebody along the way had informed on me. The local police picked me up and, after releasing me on bail, gave me a date to appear at the Old Bailey.

Tony took me up to London, but this time was unable to stay. It was a nice surprise to see Joan Askew at the court. It seemed to me, even at that time when I was still not a Christian, that God always brought someone along to give me the support that I needed. I had pleaded guilty to the charge and, even though I knew I was only on the fringe of all that had been happening, felt there was a distinct possibility that I might receive a custodial sentence. It was good when I went up before the judge to find him surprisingly sympathetic. He told me he was going to give me a chance, one last chance. He recognised the fact that I had moved to Devon to get away from the drugs scene, and so I ended up with probation. Now I was able to go back to Devon knowing that all the court cases were cleared up and that there were no more worries, or so I thought at the time.

A lot was happening in the local area. We still occasionally went to the large community church, but this was a few miles away from where we lived and it had been decided recently that there should be a separate church more locally based. As a result of this decision an elder was appointed and the church started to meet in a hall in the local village. I think the idea was that this new elder would be in charge of the church, but would work in relationship to the larger church that we had previously been going to.

I continued going to church, and I continued to

sit there while people sang and praised and while people preached, and yet somehow the personal message was still not getting through to me. I had, however, got used to the idea of being in the company of Christians and despite the fact that they, like everybody, had their faults, I could see that there was genuine loving commitment in them.

I was still popping over to see John and Barbara regularly. John talked a lot about drugs and such things, and in a sense I enjoyed this, but in another way I began to realise that there was just no Christian sincerity in him at all. He was going to all the meetings. He seemed to be really alive in God and had even been giving his testimony and yet I began to see that it was one big act that he immediately assumed in front of anyone who was a genuine Christian. As soon as the Christian left he went back to his normal behaviour.

By now, Tony was starting to take a firm line about John. He had been seen driving around with no tax on his car, and seemed to be telling lies over even the smallest matters. This may not seem very wrong to someone who isn't a Christian, but I could see that it did cause a problem in the fellowship. John was claiming to be a Christian and yet was doing these things. Because of these problems the elder, with friends, had come to see John quite a few times and I was always sickened by the facile way in which John would convince them that he was doing nothing wrong, and then laugh behind their backs immediately they left. Even though I still wasn't a Christian myself, I didn't like to see sincere people being used and deceived in this way. I think I also recognised that being a Christian demanded a different kind of lifestyle from that of the non-Christian.

Gradually, because of this conflict between John and Tony, tensions arose between Tony and the elder in the fellowship. I myself was torn between two worlds. I liked the Christians and yet I wasn't a Christian. I liked talking to John about the past, and yet I was beginning not to like him very much as a person. It seemed that everything was coming to a head.

My regular routine at that time was to get up quite early, walk down to the local village health centre, pick up my drugs and then slowly wander back. This happened every day of the week except Sundays, as on Saturday I would pick up two days supply of drugs to cover me for the weekend.

One Saturday morning, before I was even out of bed, I heard a knock on the door and went down to answer it. I was very surprised to see Barbara, John's wife. She told me that they had come to give me a lift down to the health centre. I felt that this was a bit odd, but nevertheless it was a lift, so I hurriedly got dressed and went out with Barbara to the car.

When I got to the car, John turned round and told me that he had broken into the local health centre the night before and cleared the place out of all the drugs there. At first I thought he was joking, as he did tend to have a habit of laughing about everything. The health centre was only a mile or so down the road and we were soon within sight of it. It was then that I suddenly realised he was serious, for I could see police cars outside the centre. John dropped me a little bit up the road from the health centre and I went in to try to get my drugs. At the reception desk I was told that there had been a break-in and that my drugs had been stolen, and that I would have to come back later in the day when they would have obtained my drugs from somewhere else.

John took me back up to his place, and then he offered me as many amps of physeptone as I wanted. It seemed crazy to me because this was the very physeptone that I was to have picked up earlier that day. I knew as soon as I accepted the drugs from him that I was now implicated in what had happened. However, I was desperate, although in the back of my mind I realised that John must have known that he was implicating me in the case.

Later that morning I went down to pick up the amps of physeptone that I was legally entitled to from the health centre.

I hung around with John and Barbara all that day. He had been taking drugs since the previous night and all through that day, so was in a bit of a state. In the end he asked me if I would go to London with him and help him to sell some of the drugs that he had stolen. Looking back on this it all seems crazy, as the people who I knew really cared for me were Jenny and Phil, Tony and Linda and others like them. Yet it was all too easy for me to forget them and allow John, who had no real concern for me, to drag me back into my old life.

Later that Saturday John and I left for London. I sensed that Barbara wasn't happy about this, but obviously there was little she could do about it. John was quite a big, strong man and he was drugged as well. I think by now she was getting a bit frightened of what was happening. When we reached London I sold some of the drugs around Piccadilly and then John took me on to see some of his friends.

By the time we were ready to return to Devon it was very late. This was John's second night without sleep and besides being very tired, he had taken drugs non-stop since the break-in. This meant that he was in a very dangerous condition and quite unfit for the three hour drive back to the country. All the way down from London I had to keep waking him up as he was constantly falling asleep over the wheel. We were about a third of the way back when, while I was digging around in my handbag and not conscious of what John was doing, he fell asleep across the wheel. Before I could do anything about it, the car had careered over to the other side of the road. All I can remember after that was flashing lights as we crashed head-on into a car coming the other way.

I was thrown forward into the windscreen which smashed on impact, but somehow I didn't go right through it. My arms got caught up in the seat or something. I still can't quite remember exactly what happened as I didn't have a seat-belt on, but something did stop me. I sat there in shock with blood pouring from my face, for a lot of the glass had imbedded itself in my face and around my eyes. My nose had been broken, although I didn't feel any pain as I was still numb from shock. The next thing I became conscious of was a woman's voice speaking to me. Because of the blood in my eyes I couldn't see anything, but I could hear this soothing, calm, compassionate voice, full of love and kindness. In the darkness this voice kept reassuring me and comforting me. She told me to keep my hands away from my face and that I would be all right. I will never forget that voice.

On the right of me John was now starting to move and he was groaning. 'I am dying, Anita,' he said. 'Typical,' I thought, demanding attention as always. It seemed to me that even now John was more concerned about himself than he was for me. I was certainly being taught a very hard lesson as to who my friends really were.

The woman continued to talk to me and comfort me in her reassuring voice. She then told me that the ambulance was coming and asked me if I could hear it. It was at this stage that I lost consciousness.

I was unconscious from that time until I got to the hospital. When I woke up doctors seemed to be putting tubes and needles all over me. I passed out again, and when I awoke found I was in a hospital ward in bed. I noticed two men sitting by my bed. They were plain-clothes policemen.

I didn't really have my wits about me and I wasn't up to answering questions. They said they would come back again when I would be more able to respond to questioning.

When they did come back they accused me of carrying out the break-in single-handedly and suggested that I was the key planner of the whole escapade. I don't know what was going on in my mind at that time, but because I felt I should protect John I named another person who, in fact, had had nothing to do with the break-in. I said that this other man had organised everything and that John and I just went along with him. I know, looking back, that it was quite illogical to name someone else in order to protect John, and yet I felt I should do something. I didn't want John to go back to prison even though I knew he wasn't a very nice person. I was later to discover that while I was unconscious John had slipped some of the drugs out of his pocket into my bag.

As time went by I began to feel guilty about trying to implicate this other person who had had nothing to do with the crime. I was in a very confused state emotionally. Again I called out to God, not really asking for help but seeking an explanation of why this was happening to me. I recognised that I had got myself into this situation and yet somehow it seemed inevitable that this sort of thing would happen to me. In desperation I phoned my mother from the hospital and while talking to her broke down in tears. I was totally unable to decide what action to take now. I didn't phone Tony or Linda, or any of the other Christians I knew, as I felt so guilty about what had happened. I thought everyone would blame me anyway. As a result of my phone-call, my mother wrote a letter to Tony to tell him that I was in hospital, and a couple of days later Tony came up to see me.

I told the whole truth to Tony and he, in turn, told me that John had been released on bail. Both Tony and myself felt that this was very strange as it was a serious offence and for John to have got out on bail would mean that he must have made a statement minimising his part in the affair. By then Tony was getting very suspicious of John and I think he had already guessed that John had made a statement implicating me.

In the end, after spending the afternoon with me, Tony had to go back home. He left saying that in the end I would have to tell the truth about what had happened and that he was pretty sure that John had no concern about me. I believed this, because as far as I knew John had made no enquiries about my health.

The elder of the fellowship and his wife had come up to see me as well. I felt there was a genuine concern there, but I also sensed that they were after information. I discovered that John had told them that I was the prime mover in this whole incident, and so obviously they were trying to check up on the things that they had been told. John belonged to the church and was a professing Christian. He had become very involved in the fellowship, but I was only nominally involved and obviously was still not a Christian. I felt hurt at the time, as I thought that this possibly influenced the way that people thought about this situation. I felt very wounded and rejected when I found out that some people seemed to have prejudged me before even learning the full facts of what had happened.

Eventually I was ready to be discharged from the hospital and two policemen came to take me. On the way out of the hospital I met the two ambulance men who had been at the scene of the accident. I asked them about the woman who had been such a great help to me. I was amazed when they told me that no one else had been there when they had arrived. Later on I asked the police about the woman and they again confirmed that there was no one there. I know that there was a person there – I had heard her voice, I had felt her hand, and I now believe that it was an angel sent from God. Understanding about situations like this often comes later, and I now understand that God was working in my life in a very practical and positive way, and that this angel was sent to help me at a time of desperate need.

11: Snatched from the flames

The journey in the police car passed quickly. I was glad to be out of hospital although I wasn't glad about my destination. I was taken to the nearest town and put into the cells underneath the police station, from which I was later brought out to see the CID. From some of the things that they were saying, I began to realise that they knew a lot more than they should and that John must have talked. I also began to realise that I could be in very serious trouble. I now knew that what Tony had suspected was true, that John had not only told the police about me, but had told lies, exaggerating my involvement.

I was told that Tony would be coming to see me later that day. I was surprised when they let him into the cell with me and allowed us to talk. He reiterated what he had said at the hospital, urging me to tell the truth. He knew definitely by then that John was trying to frame me for this job, and yet even at this stage my false sense of loyalty led me to try to protect the man who had nearly got me killed and had led me into this situation in the first place!

Permission was eventually given for Tony to read John's statement to me, although I myself was not allowed to look at it. I then understood fully what was going on, and after Tony had read out some of the lies that John had told about me I realised it was stupid to continue with this deception. But even then I didn't tell the whole truth, as I still didn't think that anyone would believe me. I didn't realise at the time that Jenny had been awake when Barbara had called for me that morning, and was willing to substantiate this by making a statement.

I learned later that Phil and Jenny's house had been searched by the police, who were looking for the drugs which had been taken from the health centre. I felt very bad about this.

Later that day I was released on bail to Tony's address and he came and took me home. The next couple of days were very difficult. There were practical problems as the cottage where Tony and his wife lived was very small and the only place I could sleep was on a put-up bed in the back passage, and besides this the rumour was going around that I was the prime mover in the break-in. This of course was ludicrous, as I would not have been physically capable of smashing a window, climbing up and then entering and forcing open cabinets and cupboards. I was very hurt that people so readily believed what John had said.

I knew that John could be very plausible for I had previously seen the way he had deceived the elders of the fellowship. He was a complex character, a mixture of weakness and apparent strength. I had seen him turn on the tears, and then the next minute laugh at the people who had responded to him. He certainly seemed able to wind people around his little finger when he wanted.

Funnily enough, the people who did believe me seemed to be the young Christians – people who perhaps knew me a bit better than the others. Somehow they were able to understand what had happened. I was glad that Jenny and Phil and another friend of Tony's wife called Claire, also believed me. This helped to make up for the hurt I was feeling through other Christians doubting me.

Although I was still a non-Christian amongst Christians I was now the centre of a lot of Christian controversy, and I know that many problems arose because of my situation.

During this period I had to go down to see the police once or twice as they wanted to interview me further concerning the offences. Even though they now knew that John had done the job they still needed to have evidence and proof. One day they wanted to take a blood test as some blood had been found at the scene of the break-in, but they were unable to get any blood from me. I was taken to a doctor but, despite all his efforts and the pain I went through, we didn't end up with a drop of blood, for most of my veins had collapsed.

The police had picked up a bag containing some of John's clothes and some other drugs, so they were gradually getting their case together.

I could see the frustrating effect that this whole situation was having upon Tony and his family, but I felt that there was nothing I could do. It is hard to describe the hurt and rejection that I felt at that time. I felt that I had been judged and condemned without a hearing by many people in the fellowship. I didn't resent them for this as I knew John was very plausible, but this did not take away the hurt.

One night, when I was staying at Tony and Linda's, we started to talk about my life and what a mess it was in. I had made yet another mistake which could possibly lead to imprisonment. I was very depressed. It seemed as though trouble followed me everywhere and there was no way I could get away from it. When I should have been strong I was weak. Here was a situation which need never have happened and yet, like a lamb going to the slaughter, I had just drifted into it without thinking about the implications or the possible results of my actions.

Tony, as always, was talking about Jesus and how God could help me, but it still didn't seem to make any sense to me. In a way I wished it could, because obviously I needed something, but in the middle of this conversation there was a knock at the door.

It was the elder of the fellowship. He came into the house somewhat warily for there had been a lot of tension between Tony and him, particularly over this situation. He sat down and, with a rather nervous smile, said, 'I've got some good news for you, John's been nicked.'

Tony seemed to explode when he realised that the elder only now believed what he had been telling him for weeks. All his built-up frustration erupted and he and the elder launched into a bitter argument. I felt caught in between as I was sitting on a couch with one on either side of me. Suddenly Tony stopped the argument and said to the elder, 'Why are we arguing in front of her when we should be praying for her?' Then he looked at me and said 'Right, Anita, I want to pray with you.'

Tony asked me to kneel down; I felt totally embarrassed at this but didn't feel I had much choice in the matter. I knelt down and he and the elder knelt down with me. I can't remember exactly what Tony prayed but I know he mentioned something about unclean spirits and binding them in the name of Jesus, and coming against Satan in the name of Jesus. After Tony had prayed he asked me if anything had happened. Indeed something had happened. There had been a stirring inside me, similar to what I had experienced at the crusade in some ways, but slightly different. I had tried to push it down; I was frightened. Many things were flashing through my mind. All the old smothering experiences of evil came back to me and with them a great fear.

Tony gave me a Bible to read, and after the elder had left I settled down into bed and started to read. I suddenly began to realise that the devil was very real, and that there was a connection between the smotherings and the devil. At that moment I prayed my first real prayer. It was simply, 'Jesus, please help me.'

Most of that night I spent awake, talking to God. There seemed to be a real battle going on within me. Perhaps the main difference between now and the other times when I called out to God, was that I was talking to Jesus as a person. I did feel that I was getting through and sensed that this was only the beginning, and that there was a lot more that had to be dealt with in my life.

When I look back on that evening I believe that the prayers that were prayed for me in the front room were preparing the way for me to respond to God. There are two scriptures which have given me more understanding of what happened. One is Romans 8:28 where it says that all things work together for good to those called according to God's purpose, but another scripture which certainly seems relevant to the way in which I became a Christian can be found in Jude v23: '. . . Save some by snatching them as from the very flames of hell itself'. As I think about all the circumstances that led up to that night, I realise that I was certainly one of those people who needed to be snatched from the flames. I believe that the only way I could have become a Christian is through the sort of situation that surrounded my conversion. I had waited some two years, living in Christian company without making any sort of move towards God, and yet now circumstances had come about which had brought me into living contact with the Living God.

It is good to know that God is able to use all things to bring people to the point of knowing Him through Jesus, and I am glad that God allowed the accident for, through the very instrument which could have killed me, I found a new life.

12: Starting to grow

The next morning I was sitting in an armchair waiting for Tony to come down. I felt numb. It had been a long night. The pressures and problems were still around me as there was still the court case and the church situation, yet somehow I was aware that something had changed inside me.

I had to get down to the health centre to pick up my drugs. Tony gave me a lift and on the way down said something which I couldn't quite understand at the time, 'Welcome to the family, sister.'

From the first stirrings of that night, and over the next couple of weeks, I began to enter into a real relationship with Jesus. That night I had made a connection of some sort and as time passed this first contact developed into a warm and solid relationship. I felt that I had come home for the first time. I had at last found my real Father and, because of Jesus, I was totally accepted. I felt that I was covered with a blanket of love which held me warm and secure.

I started reading the Bible, and the more I read the more excited I became. I could understand what was written in there and Jesus became more and more real to me as a person. Even more important, I knew that He understood me.

Prayer came almost naturally. In the past I had been shouting at God but somehow never feeling I had got through, and yet now I was connecting. I was no longer angry, bitter and frustrated. I knew that I was communicating and again, more importantly, knew that God was communicating with me. There were a couple of times when I heard actual words which I believed came from Jesus Himself. Very quietly and softly He was saying, 'I love you', and this gave me a tremendous feeling of warmth and security.

However, everything wasn't a bed of roses. I still had to sleep in the back passage and I was still fearful of the dark. I didn't like being on my own, particularly at night.

There were also difficulties with the elder of the fellowship, who was still inclined to believe that I was involved in the break-in at the health centre. I was very hurt and confused over this and distressed when Linda came into conflict with the elder, through her defence of me. I felt sad that once again I seemed to be causing trouble and yet, looking back on the situation, I realise that God does work in all things. I didn't feel now like running back to London; I was facing up to the situation even though it was very difficult. Eventually, because of the tensions that had arisen, Tony and Linda were to leave the area, which in the long term worked out very well. It is good to know that God is always in control, and that ultimately He worked this situation out for the good of all the people involved.

Obviously, sleeping in the back passage was not ideal either for myself or for Tony and his family. I was glad when an opportunity came up for me to be able to move to a caravan site just the other side of the village. Tony, at one time, had worked in a breaker's yard and the caravan had come to me through one of the people who had worked with him.

I packed all my belongings and, even though I loved Tony and the family very much, I felt very glad to be stepping out and getting a place of my own at last.

For the last couple of years I had been living with families and now I was glad of this opportunity of looking after myself and having a bit of privacy. Besides this I wanted to be on my own with Jesus and have time to read my Bible in peace and have more control of my own life. So I quite looked forward to the day when I would move. It seemed like another step along the road to full recovery.

Despite my problems with the leadership at the fellowship, I was getting very close to individuals. One of these, another woman called Linda, had offered me a job two days a week cleaning her house. I was very grateful for this for many reasons. Not only did it mean that I didn't have to be in my caravan on my own all the time, but it also meant that I was being trusted.

Linda owned a paper round and was out quite a lot on her rounds. There were often hundreds of pounds from the rounds lying around the house. It was so good to know that I was being trusted with all this money around, and I really felt that I needed this after my recent experiences.

Life started to look up for me. I still had the court case to go through but by now most people realised that John had done the job, and it was generally accepted that I hadn't been involved. When this became known the attitude of the church and the leadership did change noticeably. I felt more and more accepted by the church, and offers began to come for help with the court case. Linda had already offered to come up and give me a reference, particu-

S.F.F.—6

larly emphasising the fact that I worked in her house where there was money available. And when I went to see the elder to ask him for a letter of reference he said that he would like to come up and speak for me himself.

Gradually things were settling down. Tony and Linda moved away and I was sad to see them go. After all, they had been a great help and support to me and if it hadn't been for their home I would never have got away from London, and probably would never have come to the Lord. But I felt that now at last I would have to stand alone and in many ways was glad about this. I felt I no longer needed protection and people to fight my battles for me. I now felt able to cope with life on my own and wanted this. Before leaving Tony had talked to me about the drugs and mentioned different ways of coming off, but at that time I wasn't ready for it. I still couldn't imagine myself ever coming off drugs.

I was starting to really get into the church services by now. I met with the local house-groups and gradually found that God was starting to sort out many of the things that had been wrong in the past. My relationship with the elder, even though it never became very close, did improve and through his offer of help with the court case I realised that God could overcome in situations like this and draw people together. The church continued to be supportive to me and there was a great movement in the area, originating from the Don Double crusade, of Christians from different churches and fellowships meeting together. I began to get to know many individual Christians both in my own church and also in the churches around the area.

In January, four months after my conversion, I was

baptised as a believer. Tony returned for the occasion to take part in the service. Although I had had many doubts and second thoughts about taking this step, it was a joyful occasion and I learnt later that the non-Christian husband of a member of our fellowship had become a Christian as a result of attending the service.

Since going down to the country I had needed to return to my clinic in London every three months or so for a check-up and chat with the social worker and doctor. I always combined this with a visit to my family. I had found since leaving London that I was really starting to build a new relationship with them. I told them that I had become a Christian, but it didn't really make a lot of difference to the way they thought about me as they knew I was still on drugs. However, it was good to have contact with them again. I felt it important not only to maintain this communication but to follow it through by seeing them as often as I could.

It was shortly after my baptism that I started to think seriously about coming off drugs, and I decided to go up to the clinic and tell them. They were obviously surprised and perplexed by my decision. Many addicts can be maintained on six amps of physeptone for the rest of their lives, and there was no physical need for me to come off. I told them that I was now a Christian, but all this drew was more puzzled looks. My family however, were delighted about my decision, particularly my mother. She came up to the clinic with me one day and they told her quite plainly that they could never imagine me coming off drugs. Despite this initial lack of encouragement, the clinic were prepared to co-operate with me, but wanted me to decide for myself just how and when I was going to start cutting down. Eventually I decided that I would cut down one amp a month. I phoned the clinic and we agreed on the date when I would come off my first amp.

Around the time of this decision much had been happening in my spiritual life. Besides having been baptised in water which had been a tremendous spiritual experience for me, I had also prayed for the baptism in the Holy Spirit. As it had been with my conversion, I couldn't understand it all at the time, but something had definitely happened to me. I felt that through being baptised in the Holy Spirit, prayer and Bible study were becoming more and more real. Usually I would pray in English, but sometimes I would slip into what is known as speaking in tongues.

It's funny how I started speaking in tongues. Usually in the morning I got up feeling sick, but one particular morning something very unusual happened. It had all started the previous night. I had gone to bed as usual, woken up and then dozed off back to sleep again when I suddenly felt as though something was falling on me. It felt like something warm and comfortable. Looking back, I believe that this was the anointing of the Holy Spirit falling on me.

When I woke up I felt so fresh and so alive and the first words I spoke were, 'I love you, Jesus.' I felt something new in my heart, a genuine feeling of love towards God. Even though I had said I was sorry for my sins I felt that God, in a very loving way, was now leading me into a deeper repentance about the sins that I had committed in the past, and also making me very aware of how sinful I still was. Yet, simultaneously, I felt a reassurance of love and acceptance. On the way down the road that morning

I was praising the Lord and suddenly I started to speak in tongues, in a new language. I had heard a lot about this at the fellowship I was going to, as people did exercise the gifts of the Holy Spirit there. I had heard people speaking in tongues before, but it was wonderful for me to be experiencing this myself for the first time.

The whole day stands out in my memory as it was a day when I had picked up my six amps of physeptone, and yet somehow I didn't get round to having a fix until much later. I was so busy praising the Lord that the time just seemed to flash by and the drugs seemed irrelevant.

In between phoning the clinic and actually coming off the first amp I was to have second thoughts. I think when anyone makes a decision for God it is difficult to carry it through. I certainly found it was easy to make the decision, and yet much harder actually to carry it through. However, I didn't go back on my word and even though I was sick the night before, mainly through fear of whether I could cope, when the actual time came I found that it was quite easy to put aside this first amp.

I also found that the next couple were quite easy. God seemed to fill me with peace, power and strength before I actually came off them so that on the actual day I stopped it had all been dealt with and I was ready.

I had kept in contact with Joan Askew, the lady who had brought coffee and sandwiches to the addicts on Piccadilly. She had been a very important link in the chain which had eventually led to my leaving London. We had seen each other occasionally when I went back to London, and I particularly remember a time when she sent me some money, as

I was utterly amazed that someone would just send money out of the blue, not expecting it back and with no strings attached. She had also sent my mother some money, and had told us at the time that she felt that God had told her to do this.

I heard that Joan was wanting a break and asked her to come down and stay with me for a week. After inviting her I had second thoughts about it and later I discovered that Joan also had some misgivings. I was a little bit frightened that we just wouldn't get on well together. A lot had changed. I was no longer on the Piccadilly scene and the relationship would be different. However, despite our fears, praise the Lord, she did eventually come down and we had a lovely time of fellowship together that week.

There is a Bible verse which says that where two or three are gathered in Jesus' name then He is in the midst, and I felt during that week that Jesus was in the midst of us in a very special way. We were both strengthened and helped during the week. Joan needed a lot of encouragement. She had been working with addicts in the 'dilly for years and had not seen many come right off drugs, so it was good to know that my life was already being used as an encouragement to someone else. While Joan was staying we were able to take the opportunity to drive over to see Tony and Linda. They were living at the time with some friends who had offered to put them up for a month or so and were hoping to move into a rented cottage soon. They seemed well, although I sensed they had suffered a lot through the experiences they had been through over the last couple of years.

Tony popped over occasionally and took me to a Prison Christian Fellowship meeting, where I was to meet various individuals who have since become friends in Jesus. I was still at that time findıng it very difficult to relate, particularly to new people. I was desperately seeking to reach out, and yet felt that people couldn't understand me or the things I was saying. I was very conscious of the fact that I was still on drugs and it was to be a long time before I felt relaxed and secure in myself when meeting new people, even if they were Christians.

I often felt that people were treating me like a child. The didn't seem to know that I was an adult, and I felt that because I had been through many things which were socially not acceptable I was treated in a different way. I was still very vulnerable and sensitive, of course, and some of this might have been just in my own mind. But there were many times when I did feel I was the *object* of ministry, but not really sharing in any real relationships and friendships.

However, as time passed, I found that as I opened up with one or two people, so they opened up with me and things started to get better as a result. Gradually I began to form good strong Christian relationships with a few individuals. I know that this was very important to me as I'm sure it is for anyone who wants to grow up as a Christian. We not only need Christian brothers and sisters, we need Christian friends and helpmates, people with whom we can share our deepest needs, and know that we can trust them. This always works two ways and I found that as I shared my own needs, so my friends were able to share with me, and a strong bond would be built in Christ.

13: A time of testing

God had done fantastic things in my life. Jesus had become a close personal friend, and the Holy Spirit had manifested Himself in and through my life. I had had wonderful experiences of God and felt very strong in my faith, and yet there was so much more to be dealt with. I had never been able to feel open enough to share many different aspects of my life, and I was coming up to a time where God was going to cut very deeply into my life. The Bible talks of the Word of God being the sword of the Spirit and I certainly felt during this next period that the surgeon's knife was at work in my spiritual life.

One day I was sitting in the caravan. I still 'mainlined' or injected my drugs straight into the vein, but that day I just hadn't been able to find a vein. I had tried to inject myself in different areas of my body and as a result I was feeling very sore, dirty and frustrated. Suddenly I was aware of Jesus being with me in a very real way in that caravan, right in the midst of all the mess. I also suddenly became aware of words being spoken to me, and I believe they were directly from the Lord: 'Your body is a temple of the Holy Spirit.' I had already heard this scripture before and knew this, and yet the words that were to follow hit me right in my heart. He said, 'You are not hurting youself now, you are hurting me more.' My immediate reaction to this was gratitude that Christ was there with me in the midst of all this mess, for by then I had blood all over me. The tears welled up in my eyes as I realised that I must indeed be hurting Him by doing the things I was doing to my body.

From that day on I no longer mainlined. To someone who isn't an addict this may not mean a lot, but most of the thrill an addict gets from fixing is through mainlining, which creates an immediate sensation. From then on I 'skin popped' which meant that I just injected myself to keep stable. I felt Jesus was pleased with this and I know that I felt very much more at peace about this decision.

Within a couple of days of this experience I was to enter into what I can only call a time of testing or refining. Recently I had been to the doctor to get some pills which were to help to relax my muscles as my body was in a bad way after all the injecting over the years. It is important to underline that the drugs that I was taking were not hallucinogenic, as I know many people claim to have weird spiritual experiences through hallucinative drugs.

Although I had been through such bad experiences, I had never actually felt like killing myself, now I started to hear voices in my head and in the caravan, urging me to commit suicide. At first I just didn't know what to do, as I was hearing specific instructions: put your head in the oven, take a lot of pills, and so on. As I was still the sort of person who didn't like to make a fuss and had somehow coped for years on my own, I didn't feel able to share what was happening to me. This carried on for days and really affected my prayer life and my Bible reading. I felt as if I was beginning to regress spiritually and even began to have second thoughts about continuing coming off drugs.

I was still going to the house-group and the church fellowship, and yet no one seemed to notice what I was going through. I felt totally alone and unable to share. I was frightened that they would feel I was just seeking attention and imagining things.

A few weeks previously, an older couple called George and Hilda had started coming to the fellowship. At that time there was a possibility that they were going to make a commitment to go there regularly. I and others were delighted about this as they were a mature couple, who had been missionaries and had been used a lot in healing and deliverance. Most of the leadership in our fellowship were young men, and some had only become Christians relatively recently.

I got up one Sunday morning as usual and went to shower to prepare myself for church. While I was in the shower I felt I was being pushed back by something. I was a bit confused by this and after the shower I sat down in a chair and gradually started to feel that I didn't really want to go to church that day. I was desperately hoping that the couple who were to pick me up wouldn't come that day, but they did turn up and somehow, although I felt very weak, I managed to get myself dressed and stagger out to the car. They dropped me at the church and I walked in and sat down.

Somehow I just didn't feel part of anything that was going on there. Even though there was so much noise around me and people were greeting each other, and presumably people spoke to me, I didn't hear them. I felt very isolated, as though I was in a cocoon in the midst of all this activity. Eventually the service started as usual with praise and worship. As always, there was a time of open worship and singing in tongues and then suddenly I started to feel tears welling up in my eyes. I didn't understand what was happening to me, but I couldn't help crying.

The elders leading the service noticed that there was something wrong, and after the worship had finished called me forward to speak to them. They wanted to pray for me, and I managed to tell them some of the things that had been happening to me, although I found it very hard to put into words. As they gathered around me to pray, George stood up and said, 'Wait a minute, I've seen this sort of thing happening before, I know what's happening to this girl.' He came forward and assumed authority in the situation, encouraging the rest of the congregation to worship and praise the Lord. He had chosen a chorus, which was very popular at the time, called 'Majesty'. The choice of that chorus was I think, very important as it really lifted up Jesus as Lord and above all things.

George's wife, Hilda, had joined him at the front and I was sitting on a chair facing the congregation. George encouraged people to gather round me and to speak in tongues, and I noticed that the others were speaking very gently, while George was speaking with authority and in a strong firm voice. Hilda had joined him in this, and it seemed apparent that these two were speaking in a different way. Gradually I began to realise that they were speaking to something in me. As George and the others continued to speak in tongues Hilda started to speak in English. Again she was speaking to something, or someone, that was inside me, and it was as though she recognised the person she was speaking to. I can't remember the exact words, because I was in a very emotional and numb state at the time, but I understood that there was something that needed to be dealt with inside me, and God was using George and Hilda to root out the evil.

Even though I was still a bit frightened, because I didn't understand just what was happening to me and around me, I felt secure in Jesus. I also felt very secure because George and Hilda seemed to have the authority that was necessary for this situation, whereas the elders, even though they were loving people, didn't really seem to know what was happening. I started to calm down and I felt that something had begun to open up inside me. George told people not to spread about what had happened in the church that morning, and I went back to my chair and sat down. Towards the end of the service George came up to me and said, 'You know it's not over yet, don't you Anita?' I was glad to hear him say this, as I myself sensed that there was more to be dealt with. I also believed that George knew what he was talking about and he was telling me that it would be all right in the end, although the worst was not over yet.

Many good things came out of this experience. I remember one young man coming up to me. He had been brought up in a Christian family although he had only become a Christian a year or so before. He said to me, 'Anita, I have never felt the Lord's presence in such a powerful way as this morning.'

I was glad to get back to the caravan that morning. I managed to get in the door and then just flopped into the armchair, where I remained for a couple of hours. I was still communicating with the Lord although I was angry with him, and resentful about what was happening to me. I felt let down and wondered why He was letting these things happen to me. Later I realised that, as we grow stronger in

Christ, He wants to deal with those things that are hindering our lives, and He only starts to deal with them when we are strong enough.

Eventually I got out of the armchair and lay on my bed. I was still thinking things through and talking to the Lord, and from time to time my frustration broke out and I would hit the bedroom wall shouting, 'Why are you doing this to me, Lord?' I suddenly remembered the times I had shouted at God before I had become a Christian and felt that I was nearly back in the same position again. At last I came to the point where I just prayed to God, 'Lord, please give me peace and rest, please help me, not my will but your will be done.'

I lay back and closed my eyes. Suddenly I felt what I can only describe as a sexual atmosphere in the room. It seemed to rekindle within me all my past sexual experiences, and was bringing me to the point of irresistible temptation. I suppose, looking back on it that God was wanting me to face up to something which I had wanted to avoid. I had not forgotten that I had been a lesbian and been involved in all sorts of things, but now it seemed that God wanted to deal really deeply with me concerning the past. His purpose was for me to be totally set free.

Some people think of becoming a Christian as an escape from reality. I certainly feel that I had to escape *into* reality, and face up to some of the nastier parts of my life so that, in facing up to them, I could grow strong and with God's strength overcome those things which had overcome me in the past.

At this point, as I was resisting what was happening to me and refusing to succumb to the atmosphere that surrounded me, I saw a vision. I saw a man at the top of some stairs. He was dressed in white and his arms were stretched out towards me, as though he was reaching out to help me and calling me upwards towards him. I must emphasise that it was when I was resisting that he appeared and offered me help. So many things had flashed through my mind during this comparatively short period of time. I had thought of Viv, and visualised myself in situations with her and felt her presence. I felt guilty and dirty and wanted to back away from it, but somehow I couldn't; I was powerless. I started to hear screaming and wailing, and then suddenly the voices sounded as though they were falling into a very deep hole.

I looked up again and this time I saw a man with a lovely face. He was just sitting there and, as I looked at him, I had a sense of warmth surrounding me, covering me and protecting me. Suddenly I felt very childlike and vulnerable and yet secure. Then I heard myself speaking and yet it wasn't the way I normally speak. It was a voice full of authority and power, and I commanded these things to get back to Hell where they belong. Not all of them had names, but one did have a name and he certainly didn't want to go. He even started arguing with me. He said, 'I've been here for years,' and suddenly I felt as though I was falling. I thought I was losing the battle. He started laughing at me, saying things like 'I've got you now'. This frightened me a bit, but I calmed down and opened my eyes. I knew that the name of this demon was the Destroyer, and suddenly a lot of things started to fall into place.

Even as a very new Christian I had recognised that my recurrent smothering incidents meant something or someone was trying to possess me and get inside me. At last I had a name for this something or someone. Jesus is sometimes referred to as

'The Light', and light exposes things that are in darkness. The light was now exposing the powers of darkness that had influenced my life, but I was also finding that at last I had the strength to fight back and, with Jesus' help, was winning the battle.

I got off the bed, picked up my Bible and sat down. As I opened it, it fell open at Daniel Chapter 10. I had never really read much in the Old Testament up to that time, but I read this chapter and found that it described Daniel's vision of 'a man'. Suddenly I began to realise that I had had a very special experience. I had seen 'the man' myself personally, just as it had happened to Daniel so many years ago. I noticed also that Daniel alone had seen this vision. He had a very special experience of God at a time when other people were afraid and certainly weren't having the same visions and experiences as he was. This made me feel very special, but also made me very aware of my uncleanness and of all that Jesus had done through His death on the cross in making me clean.

Some half an hour later, I was still sitting on the chair, and reading the Bible when I heard a knock on the door. A Christian friend of mine who had been a missionary, working in Zambia, had come to see how I was. It was good to see Jean. I really felt God had sent her along to me, as she was so excited about what was happening to me and seemed fully to understand. As I shared things that I felt God had showed me from the Bible, she was very encouraging and we had a really good time of fellowship. It is wonderful the way that God can send someone to us at just the right time and I am certain that God sent Jean along that afternoon. I am sure there would have been many who would not have understood what was happening, yet Jean did.

Jean mentioned that one of the elders and his wife wanted to see me. It was the same elder with whom I had had problems in the past. They were apparently very concerned about me because of what had happened in the service that morning, and had passed on a message to Jean that they would like to see me sometime soon. That evening Jean took me to see them. I was still very uneasy in the presence of this man, and when I shared the experience that I had had I felt there was a total lack of understanding.

On the way back I shared with Jean that I was still a bit worried concerning the last demon who had named himself 'The Destroyer', and I was afraid that it wasn't over yet. Jean suggested that I should go and see the elder again, and perhaps meet with one or two of the other elders, so that I could share with them and they could pray for me. I was a little bit worried about this but I did go and after sharing with them found that they were wanting to understand and willing to minister to me. They prayed for me and I did feel after their praying that something had happened. I was beginning to see that God was using me to build up other people. I was very glad for the unique experiences I was having on my own, and yet I was grateful that God, even at this stage in my life, was able to use what was happening to me to be of benefit to the body of Christ generally.

Near the beginning of these spiritual experiences, I had started to have second thoughts about coming off drugs. I now found that I again had reassurance from the Lord and was determined to come off drugs completely. Jean offered to put me up for a couple of days during this period and I was very grateful for this. It was good to have someone who understood me and with whom I could share totally and openly. It was very important to me to have the offer of this support, particularly through a critical phase like this. I stayed for a few days and then I went back home to the caravan and settled back into my old routine.

I felt physically and mentally exhausted. After a physical operation one needs time of recuperation, and I certainly felt that the spiritual operation I had been through had been rigorous enough for me to need a time of recuperation. Later, as I read the Bible, I saw many scriptures referring to testings and trials and I believe that this was a real time of testing for me. I am sure that people with backgrounds like mine need to go through these times of testings and trials, as the goal of Jesus is that we will not only become Christians but will grow up to be strong and mature individuals in Christ.

It seemed that I was now over this time of testing and that God was now blessing me and encouraging me. Within a day or so of being back home I had another vision. I was relaxing in the afternoon and suddenly I saw this picture of a beautiful leaf. It seemed to have dew falling on it and I saw it as a symbol of being refreshed, renewed and cleansed. It was a tremendous encouragement.

As I look back at this period I don't think I would have ever voluntarily gone through such experiences, and yet I believe that God must have known that I was strong enough to cope with them. It was good to know that I had a Father who was determined to help me to come to terms with all that was wrong in my life. I felt that whatever had been inside me was now gone, and I was new and strong and ready to go on in Jesus.

The last smothering attack I had before this was when I was at my mother's. Even then I felt that I had more strength in me, and instead of the presence coming at me it was backing away. This was the last time I was to suffer this sort of attack. Since the time of the experiences I have described I have been totally free, praise the Lord! Not only have I been free from the attacks that I have had in my past, but I have also been able to minister deliverance to other people who have been under satanic attack. A scripture that has become very relevant to me is in 2 Corinthians 1: 3–7. It says there that as God comforts us in our affliction, so we become a comfort to other people with the same comfort with which God has comforted us.

14: Freedom

Part of being a Christian is going through different stages of growth, as God not only wants to deal with different aspects of our lives related to the past, but wants to build us up with new growth so that we can become brand new people, as the Bible promises us. I had now faced up to one very difficult area of my life and felt that God had really helped me through it.

The court case had come and gone. This was to be my last court case and I remember that day very clearly. Linda and the elder who had offered to speak for me had come with me to the court. Tony had met us there and the four of us sat down in a coffee bar underneath the courts. Tony had to go off to visit somebody in prison, and the elder and Linda sat with me waiting to go up and speak on my behalf. Of course I was quite used to being in court. The elder, however, and particularly Linda, had not had many dealings with the courts and were very nervous concerning their contributions.

On surrendering my bail, I was put in the cells underneath the court. I had had time, of course, to think about what was happening. The difference between this time and the many other times that I had been waiting to appear before the courts was that first of all I had Jesus with me, so I was no longer on my own, and secondly that if I was released there was a life to go back to and to go on with.

Obviously I didn't want to go to prison, and yet I was at peace because I felt Jesus was very close to me in that cell while I was waiting. I somehow knew that whatever happened I would be all right, even if it did mean going to prison. The charge that I was up for was receiving the stolen drugs which John had taken from the health centre. In itself it was not a very serious offence but, coupled with my record, it could mean another prison sentence for me.

At last the time came for me to be taken up to the court. Here I was standing yet again in the dock, with prison officers on either side of me, facing the judge. As I looked around the court I saw Linda and the elder who were waiting to speak for me. My lawyer stood up and said that there were people in the court who were willing to speak on my behalf. I think the most impressive thing for me in this court case was seeing Linda, who was not used to the courts and was obviously feeling very nervous, standing there willing to speak for me. I really appreciated this as I knew what it cost her. I also had a solicitor who was a Christian and it was good to know that God's people were involved in so many different parts of society. After all these people had said their pieces the judge looked up at me. He said he wasn't sure whether he should give me another chance, but had decided that he would give me just one more chance and would put me on probation. In the split second between him saying that he wasn't sure about giving me another chance and then saying he would put me on probation, I really felt that I would go down for a prison sentence.

I sensed that this was the last time I would be in court and it was a good feeling. Obviously I was very relieved and was glad to get through the procedures of signing the forms in which I agreed to be on probation, and to be officially released. I was soon on my way home.

It seemed that almost everything connected with my past was gradually falling away. I still had my last amp to come off, but was now well prepared for coming off completely. I had had many offers of support from various individuals in the body of Christ, both from my church and other churches. Many had offered to put me up for that last week to give the moral and physical support that they felt would be necessary. I decided that I didn't really want to be in a home where there would be children or lots of people around, so I decided to take Jean up on her offer and went to stay with her.

In many ways this was the most important amp of physeptone. It was the last one, but somehow there wasn't a massive pressure around giving it up. It seemed as though I was just entering into something that had been accomplished already. I felt that the most important thing that had happened to me had been the deliverance experience and this had been the key thing in God's eyes. Now this was behind me I felt that the amps were just going to fall away, like leaves falling off the trees in autumn.

The day came when I went to the health centre to pick up my very last amp. I went through the usual procedure, but somehow, it seemed silly even to bother to inject it. After I had injected it I just knew that this was the end. It seemed strange that this happened so naturally, for I had been fixing for some seventeen and a half years except during prison sentences, yet here it was – my last fix.

I went to Jean's that evening and stayed overnight. The next morning I felt very weak and a bit sick. Jean had offered to take me out and as we sat in the cafe I felt I would hardly be able to help myself up again. My body, of course, was reacting to being without drugs. My liver was hurting and my head was pounding. On getting home I did something that is very unusual for someone who had just come off drugs. I told Jean I was going upstairs to lie on my bed, and I fell into a deep sleep for seven hours. I feel this was the Holy Spirit preparing me for the immediate future and helping me to be rested and strengthened.

The next few days were difficult. I still felt Jesus very much with me, but I felt cold and was shaking and going through all the normal symptoms of drug withdrawal. Also, of course, I couldn't eat. It was good to have Jean around. She was very much the instrument of God during this period, quietly supportive, understanding and yet not intrusive. Obviously she and many others were praying for me during this time.

Except for that seven hours of deep sleep I didn't sleep much during those first few days. I had been praying with Jean, and on my own, but suddenly, on the third day without drugs, I felt as if I was totally released. I felt an excitement stirring inside me as I sensed it was all over emotionally, if not physically. I still had another month to go before I could sleep properly, and before I no longer felt cold, but it never entered into my head that all I needed to do was to get some drugs again and I would be all right. It seemed that the only way I could look now would be forward. I realise, as I look back, that God was using many human instruments, both in praying and caring for me. So much of my time had been spent thinking about the court case and about this final amp. Here I was now, with Jesus, clear of drugs and except for the remaining few physical symptoms, ready to go on as a Christian. It was good to be free of the web that had ensnared me for so many years.

Somehow I knew that I wouldn't stay for much longer in this area where I had been living. I felt that this was the place where God had wanted me to grow as a Christian and, like most healthy children, I felt that now the time had come for me to leave home.

I had seen Tony and Linda a few times and knew that Tony was involved in prison work, and I felt that I would like to be closer to them so that I could become involved in the same work.

Again, a practical miracle happened as the area of East Devon where Tony lived was quite exclusive and it didn't look as though it would be possible for me to get accommodation at all. However, a friend of mine had learnt about a caravan that was available. It was a lovely place a beautiful view from the window and it seemed ideal for me.

With great excitement I packed my things and waited for friends to come over and pick me up. They took me to the caravan, and I was all set to start another stage of my Christian life.

15: Intensive training

I was soon settled into my little caravan. It was situated at the top of a hill, for I always seemed destined to have a long walk from where I lived to the nearest point of civilisation. Perhaps the Lord wanted to build up my strength. It was about a mile and half from a small village.

In some senses my physical isolation was good, because I was well away from Tony and Linda, far enough for me to be independent and lead my own life, which I felt was essential at this time. At first I didn't really miss the Church fellowship. The fellowship had been my spiritual birthplace and, now I had left home, I was quite excited looking forward to a new life on my own.

Tony and Linda now had another woman, Carole, staying with them. She was from the drug scene in Bristol and had been a prostitute for four years. I was to learn quite a few lessons about my own relationship with the Lord through meeting her. She, like myself, had been involved in drugs for quite a while and, of course, I wanted to help her. There were certain areas where I did feel I was helping her a lot but I also discovered that I wasn't quite as strong as I thought I was. I suppose part of the reason for this was that I had been staying in a country community where I was not in contact with people from my old scene. I am convinced that God takes us through times like this so that we can learn our strengths and weaknesses, and I certainly did over the next few weeks.

I feel it was good of the Lord to bring Carole across my path as I had always felt, especially after becoming a Christian, that if I ever did get clear of drugs I would want to help other people. I was beginning to learn that helping other people was sometimes very hard, but it was good to be learning and it was good to be having my faith stretched. I soon realised that part of helping other people was to bear strains voluntarily in one's own life. I suppose this is taking up the cross daily and following the Lord, as the Bible puts it. I have heard many Christians talk about 'dying to oneself' and I think this is what it's all about.

Besides meeting Carole, I also started to get involved in evangelistic work in the nearby town. Part of the ministry was the running of an open coffee bar two afternoons a week. People from all different backgrounds used to come here, particularly people who had been involved in drugs or been in prison. I was soon to learn quite a few lessons in this situation.

I know that we can learn many things from people expounding the Bible, and it's very important to hear and receive teaching from each other in the Christian body. But I believe that there are many things that God wants to teach us directly, through the Holy Spirit, and these are often very down-to-earth things which happen in our everyday lives.

At first, when I went to the coffee bar, I quite enjoyed the work and Carole would come with me sometimes. I found myself working with Betty, one of the women who was part of the team ministering at the coffee bar. One would have thought, after the life I had led, that I would have become unshockable, but unfortunately I was soon to be shocked in this Christian situation. Betty was married with four children, two of about seven or eight years old, and two boys of seventeen and fourteen. She had been baptised in the Spirit and involved in these churches for about twenty years. She certainly knew all the live fellowships around the area and at different stages had gone there with her husband. I used to pray with her and it wasn't long before she was sharing things with me which I found very difficult to handle.

Despite being a married woman, she was sleeping with some of the younger men who were coming to the coffee bar for help. I was very shocked to discover this and didn't know what to do. I confided it to Tony and his advice was to withdraw from the situation. He shared a scripture from Galatians 6: 1, which says that we ought to try to help someone who is in sin, but should watch ourselves that we should not be tempted.

At first I wasn't inclined to withdraw as I felt I wanted to help Betty, but gradually I began to see that I couldn't help her. I realised that if all the skilled counsellors who had dealt with both her and her husband through the years had not been able to help, then there was something between her and God that needed to be sorted out.

I found it a very difficult decision to withdraw from this relationship and very confusing that a woman who knew the Lord, and had experienced God in her life over such a long period, could openly and actively be encouraging young non-Christians into sin. I didn't condemn her but I didn't understand.

Tony did try to warn the leadership of the coffee

bar about this situation, but somehow they didn't seem to want to know. They said that they were trying to help Betty, but I felt that the damage she was doing in the lives of these young men was too high a price to be paid. However, she did know the Lord and I knew He could help, and I didn't want to condemn her, for who was I to condemn anyone.

As I look back over this period I can see that I was definitely deepening my relationship with the Lord. I was being put into responsible situations where I had to make decisions of a kind which I had never had to make before and I found it very difficult and emotionally draining.

My relationship with Carole continued to develop and gradually it emerged that there were things in her life which needed dealing with. Tony and Linda had prayed with Carole over some specific areas of her life in relationship to emotional healing, and different strands of the past which seemed to be tying her down. However, something else started to surface.

Carole had been involved for many years with tarot cards, seances and other aspects of the occult. I realised that this was a situation where she needed deliverance and, after sharing this with Tony, we decided that we would pray for her.

The Holy Spirit was certainly putting me through an intensive teaching course. I was learning much about myself and beginning tentatively to step out into realms which I had never entered before. I remember the night Tony and I prayed for Carole. We claimed scriptures such as Matthew 18:18 where it says that where two or three bind something on earth it is bound in heaven, and where two or three loose something on earth it is loosed in heaven.

Quite a long period of prayer was necessary, and at various stages I wondered whether I was out of my depth in praying for Carole in this way. However, something did happen that night and Carole experienced a new release in her life. It was so good to be used by God, but I was beginning to feel the strain and tension that comes with this type of ministry. I would advise anyone stepping out in this realm to make sure that they are alongside a more mature Christian, experienced in such ministry, and also to be prepared for spiritual counter-attack and the physical and emotional strain that comes with this work.

I continued to go up to London quite regularly to see my parents. My relationship with them was growing stronger. Obviously they could see that I was off drugs and I knew that my brother sometimes read Christian books, but somehow the personal message didn't seem to be able to come through to them. However, it was good to keep in contact with them and to know that our relationship could only get better.

It was on one of these trips that I came across a girl whom I had met previously through Tony. She had come down for the weekend for some counselling and help with Tony and Linda and returned to London. She was from a drugs background, and was bisexual. She had been a Christian some two or three years by now, had been baptised in the Holy Spirit and was part of a very live charismatic church in London. She was one of many people I was to meet who seemed to go up and down like yo-yos over the years, one minute being radiant in Christ and the next being back into the drugs scene.

Again, I found myself out of my depth in a situation where I desperately wanted to help. I found that instead of helping her I was in danger of being pulled back into my old ways. I knew at a certain stage in our relationship that if I didn't pull away I would actually fall all the way back, so I was starting to learn that there were still certain areas of weakness which I would have to protect for quite a long time. Despite the fact that God had delivered me from many things in my past there were still areas which I had to be careful over. I suppose part of growing up as a Christian is recognising that one has weaknesses as well as strengths, and I was certainly learning about my weaknesses in a very real way. I am glad, however, that I wasn't over-protected as I feel that I had to learn these lessons for myself, with the guidance and help of other Christians.

I still occasionally went with Tony to Prison Christian Fellowship groups, as Tony was much involved with working for this organisation. Part of their ministry is setting up prayer and care groups for prisons. I was beginning to get to know more and more individuals involved in Prison Christian Fellowship around the country, and I would occasionally give my testimony as well. I am glad that I didn't share my testimony in the earlier days as I knew many people with backgrounds similar to my own have been encouraged to testify before they were ready for it and have sometimes come unstuck. But as I now shared my testimony here and there, I would come across people who had been praying for me, sometimes for years. I particularly remember an old couple whom I had never met before, who told me that they had been earnestly praying for me over a two year period. I began to realise the importance of sharing what God had done for me, as so many people had been faithful in their prayers for me.

By now Carole who, like me, had started off by sleeping on the floor in the back room of Tony's house, had moved into a caravan which was parked in their drive-way. She had only been a Christian for some three or four months yet already I could see that God was working very deeply in her life. It was great to be a part of what was happening to her and to know that I had a friend who understood me. I really felt that God had supplied Carole for me although He was also able to use me to be of help to her. So all in all I had gone through a very intensive training period, and perhaps this was preparation for what was to come next.

many people had been [illegible] graves [illegible]

By now [illegible] who, like [illegible] had [illegible] off [illegible] sleeping on the floor in the back room of [illegible] house, [illegible] which was [illegible] in [illegible]. She had only been [illegible] for some three or four months [illegible] already [illegible] God was working very deeply in her [illegible] what was happening to her [illegible] really [illegible] applied [illegible] He was also able to [illegible] and perhaps that [illegible] was [illegible]

16: The tour

For a long time Tony had had the seeds of an idea for a presentation. His basic plan was that we should do a tour and, using the music from an LP he had made, endeavour to reach out to many people in the name of Jesus with the message of hope. Another burden of Tony's was that the Church should be educated and edified concerning the social problems in our society, particularly with reference to drugs, prisons and children in care. He hoped that he could get together a presentation which would combine educating and challenging the Church with reaching out in the name of Jesus.

At first this presentation was no more than an idea but then Tony made contact with two men from Daylight Publishing Company who offered to help with promoting what had begun to be known as the 'Life Presentation'. Also we had come across a lovely dancer called Anne, who was gifted in interpreting Christian music, so gradually all the different pieces were coming together. We had the music and we had the narrative theme which Tony's wife Linda was going to read. This contained information about prisons, children in care, drugs and so on, and discussed the roots of the problems and the spiritual principles involved in what was going on in our society. We also had our testimonies.

On meeting Ian and Dougal, the two men from

Daylight Company, we suddenly began to realise that we were taking on quite a massive project. In the end we settled on six venues, going from Newcastle to Glasgow, then to Birmingham, London and Chelmsford and ending up in Bournemouth. This would mean that we would have to do meetings every night over a six day period and travel some fourteen hundred miles.

Another important point which Tony insisted on, and with which I agreed, was that ex-prisoners themselves should minister, as he often felt that ex-prisoners were just looked upon as people who could give testimonies but not do a lot more. He always had this vision for the release into ministry of young people and others who were not usually considered for such work, and felt that there was much undiscovered spiritual potential in many individual members of the body of Christ.

The tour was to take place in Prisoners' Week, which is a time, usually falling in the second week of November, when many churches promote the needs of prisons through posters and leaflets. Tony felt that this was a good time to hold the presentation as it would give individual Prison Christian Fellowship groups an evening to centre on.

By now there was quite a team of us. I was feeling excited and yet a little bit frightened as I would have to give my testimony six nights running and also travel long distances, and even though God had delivered me from so much I still felt very weak physically. However, I did realise that this was a challenge to me, as here was an opportunity for me to do something for the Lord and to reach out in the name of Jesus to many who were like I used to be.

The team was now made up of Tony and Linda, Ian and Dougal, Joseph and Laura, Malcolm, an ex-prisoner from the Bournemouth area, Anne, the dancer, Carole and myself. Carole was coming along just to help on the practical side and because Tony did not want her left on her own when we all went away. Tony and Linda were bringing their two children along, too, and another woman called Helen was to join us later. Her job would be to help to keep a check on all the finances.

I knew there were a lot of problems in setting up a national tour like this on the restricted budget that we had, but at last all the posters had gone out, the arrangements were made and we were all set to go.

We had had a sort of rehearsal the day before leaving and I remember walking into the room and seeing a great mound of cables and equipment. I had found it very difficult to give my testimony in a 'practice' situation as the things I was sharing seemed so personal to me. We all gathered together at about three in the afternoon and loaded the equipment onto a lorry, but most of us went on in another minibus. We were on our way to our first destination, which was Newcastle.

We didn't arrive until the early hours of the morning and I was absolutely shattered, but I still couldn't sleep. I was terribly nervous because I knew that I was going to give my testimony in a very open and public way the next day. I wasn't sure how many people would be there, and it was the first time that I had really opened myself to people publicly. In one way I certainly wanted to share what God had done for me, as I knew there were so many out there in desperate need, but I was still afraid to open up to people. There was a constant battle going on within me. There were also the fears of drying up, and of not being able to express myself as I would wish to. I felt totally out of my depth.

The next morning we gathered at the house of Brian Stevenson, the Northern Regional Co-ordinator for Prison Christian Fellowship, who was very encouraging towards us all. His wife and family gave us a meal, and later that day we went on to the church where we were to do the presentation.

After unloading all the equipment, there didn't seem to be much for most of us to do, so Carole, Linda and I went off to a café where we had lunch together. We joined the others later that afternoon for a lovely tea that had been set out for us by local Christians, and we were grateful for their encouragement. We prayed together, and then we were ready for the presentation.

This was the night when all the teething troubles with the equipment had to be worked out, and all of us were very nervous. Tony had started off by singing a song about a girl who had died on drugs, and I knew I was to follow. When he had finished singing I went forward to the microphone, even then not knowing what I would be able to say. We had worked out some sort of order for the presentation. Basically we were to cover the 'negative' side for the the first half, and the 'positive' for the second half. This meant I was to give my testimony in two different parts, the first leading up to the point of my conversion and the second on becoming a Christian and going on with the Lord.

Somehow I got through the first part. I don't remember exactly what I said, but I know it was less than I wanted to say. In the second half I described how Christ had found me, and the different things He had done in my life, and yet all the time I was feeling frustrated as I wanted to share so much more. My nerves seemed to be letting me down, and I didn't seem to have the liberty to share in the way that I would have liked.

Most of us that evening were feeling that the whole presentation had been a mess, but then right at the end, when we were all feeling discouraged, Brian Stevenson stood up and was really enthusiastic about the evening and thanked us for coming. This was a tremendous encouragement for us, as we had all been feeling we had let people down.

After a good night's sleep we set off on the road again bound for Glasgow. It was good to be travelling. We had a chance to talk and share and pray about the different things that had happened the night before. Also it was a relief to have things going on to take my mind off the next hurdle of speaking that night.

The presentation in Glasgow, in a very large hall, certainly seemed to go better and, even though there was no direct response during the meeting, Tony did pray with someone afterwards. This was a young girl who was from a similar background to Tony and me and I felt that we were able to be of help to her. Other people came up to share and talk after the presentation was over, and I was very encouraged by the number of people who told me how blessed they had been through my testimony and asked for advice and help.

The next day we made our way down to Birmingham, where again we were in a massive hall. We had taken the perhaps presumptuous step of hiring the Methodist Central Hall. Birmingham for me was to be the real low spot of the tour, a hurdle which I was very glad, with God's help, to be able to get across. By now I was emotionally and physically totally exhausted and felt I was very much under satanic attack. I had a blinding headache from tension and felt I just had to rest. I wasn't even sure that I would be able to speak that evening. Obviously everyone else was tired as well by that time, and I was very aware that I was in a real spiritual conflict.

When we went out on the stage there were very few people, scattered here and there around the vast auditorium, and none of us felt very comfortable. Somehow, with people praying for me, I had managed to get myself onto the platform and was waiting to speak. I think that night I really did break through in a new way. Despite the fact that I was so physically and emotionally drained I spoke in a much clearer and more precise way than previously. I had been ready to give up in the afternoon, but somehow God had poured His strength into me and I was able to stand up and share in a very difficult situation.

Again it was encouraging, even in a presentation which we felt was a total failure, to meet individual Christians who were helped or blessed by what they had seen and heard.

The next day we all felt rather chastened. We felt Birmingham had been a bit of a disaster for us and were dreading the next venue, which was London. Here we had taken the large step of faith, or presumption (and we were not sure which), of booking the Central Hall, Westminster.

Tony had gone ahead with the lorry and equipment so that he could start unloading it at the other end. On arriving there we found, to our horror, that to get to the Central Hall we had to unload the equipment at the back, walk through a long corridor, put the equipment in some lifts and then carry it all through a few doorways and steps to the stage. In our tired and low state I don't know how we would have managed alone, but we were greatly encouraged when some Christians turned up, all fresh and full of vigour, willing and able to help us to get the equipment onto the stage. Members of Prison Christian Fellowship had also arrived earlier and had already prepared some sandwiches for us. And it was best of all to see Joan Askew's smiling face as she came and welcomed us.

This presentation was the most important one for me. My sister had said that she would come and I was looking forward to that, although I was nervous to think that she would be out there listening to me. Suddenly we were all set to go. After our experience at Birmingham, we were all just relying totally on the Lord. Far more people had turned up at this venue and the whole centre block was full. It turned out to be a night when everything came together. I was able to share and talk and there were no technical hitches, and there was a tremendous response from the people there.

Towards the end Tony had been sharing and had given an appeal and we were into our closing song, when a young woman walked forward. Tony motioned to me that I should go down and speak to her. I went down off the stage and started talking to her while Tony and the rest of the team finished the song. She opened up concerning her fears of things of the Holy Spirit, particularly the baptism in the Holy Spirit and speaking in tongues. I really felt that God had wanted *me* to speak to this woman as this was an area about which I was very sensitive. We were able to share and I eventually prayed with her that God would take away the fear in her life.

Many other people came forward that night and it was lovely to look around and see so many individuals being prayed for and needs being met. It seemed that we had somehow got through the testing time and were now reaping some of the fruits. It was wonderful to realise that I had been able to be an encouragement to this young woman and others who had been there. I suddenly noticed a young lad who was sitting with his parents. Most of the young people had drifted off by now, and I just felt that I should go over and speak to him. He wasn't a Christian and, after some conversation, I asked if he wanted Jesus to come into his life. He indicated that he would like this, so we prayed together. I know that night many beecame Christians and others were helped in various ways as people came forward, almost without any urging. I caught a glimpse of how God could use me and it was certainly wonderful to be used personally as an instrument of salvation for that young lad.

Another added bonus for me was that my sister had come to the presentation although she had arrived late. I caught a glimpse of her in the break and I realised that she had brought along with her, not only my sister-in-law, who was a high-class prostitute in London, but also a man who was one of her clients. I certainly felt that these presentations were for people just like this. I don't know what effect the presentation had on them, as they left quite early, but I did pray that something may have got through to them.

It was good of the Lord to give us this encouragement, and we slept much easier that night. We were to go to Chelmsford the next day, and after staying the night with local Christians we were all set to go on the road again. Perhaps it is appropriate at this point to mention the extra blessing that we derived through staying in the homes of so many different Christians around the country. It was really good to know that people were open and willing to put us up and we were doubly blessed through being able to share with them on a private and personal level.

The presentation at Chelmsford went very well and I found I was able to share more of what God had done for me. I felt I was branching out from just giving my testimony and it was good to be gaining confidence, although I was still very nervous.

Our last presentation was to be in Bournemouth the next day. It was based in an old Anglican church, so the setting was very different from many of the others we had been in. I thought it was significant that we had been in a Baptist church, two Methodist Central Halls, a Pentecostal church and now an Anglican one – so many different venues in one week, all arranged by different members of the Body of Christ.

A dear friend of ours, Jill Thomas, who was the Prison Christian Fellowship group leader for that area, had prepared lunch for us. The presentation went well and I think we were all glad to know that after this last evening we would be off home.

When I look back on the 'Life' tour I see it as a time of deepening. I certainly found that I had unexpected reserves of energy and strength, although I also learnt to lean totally on the Lord each time I had to speak. I began to catch a glimpse of the ministry that I could have in inspiring and encouraging others, by praying with people and through my testimony and life. It was good to know that there were at least a few people who had become

Christians as a direct result of the tour. And I was very much aware that even though I had been used personally, I had been very much part of a ministering team. I know all of us look back on the tour as a time of learning, both in the spiritual and practical realms.

I think I also realised how precious my testimony was. God had given me one which could bring hope to other people, particularly those in my own situation or those who feel they are beyond help. I began also to realise that giving one's testimony is not just a matter of standing up and speaking. We enter into spiritual warfare as we open up about ourselves, and give other people the opportunity of opening themselves up to God.

Yes, I was glad to get home, but this tour had given me a glimpse of the needs that existed around the country, and an insight into how God might use me in the future.

17: A source of encouragement

I soon settled back to my home routine. Later that year Tony was thinking of opening up a coffee bar under the auspices of the YMCA. I was quite excited about this idea as it would mean an everyday contact with young people in the area and a base from which we could plan further 'Life' presentations. Also it would give me something positive to do with my day.

I was now at a stage where many of my relationships with people were changing, and I felt that as I was maturing as a Christian, I needed more space and freedom in which to develop. I was also concerned to find out the Lord's plans for my future. So when an opportunity arose for me to go to London for three months, I felt that it would be good for me to spend this time away from my situation. It would help me to see things in perspective. The Lord supplied the money, and I arranged to stay with my parents.

I learnt many things during that time in London. I was able to share at a couple of meetings, and I met with individual Christians around London, and attempted to reach out in Jesus' name to people from a similar background to my own. I think one of the main things I learnt from this time was how much I had going for me back in the country with Tony, Linda, Carole and others. I feel it really confirmed to me that that was where I should be, and because of this I felt that the whole London trip was worthwhile. Another thing I learnt from this time was that I no longer had to avoid the drug scene. It is wonderful to know that Jesus does a total and complete job when He delivers someone. There was no longer any question of my desperately staying out of situations where I could be tempted, for the whole desire for drugs had gone. I was able to live in London without feeling any pressure at all to go back on drugs.

Another important lesson I learnt there was my duty and responsibility to my family, although I found it difficult living at home in a non-Christian environment. I only had one brother living at home now, and he had already been in hospital for a couple of operations on his heart. He was a gruff sort of lad, with a very rough exterior, but a soft centre. I knew he still had a Bible in his drawer next to his bed and I knew, despite what he said, that sometimes he did think about God.

My father was much the same. Unfortunately he was out of work, which really affected him very harshly. He was one of those men who could work day in, day out, and not even think about it. Besides this, he was a very taciturn man so it was very difficult to communicate with him about God. My mother, on the other hand, could talk and talk and talk and yet somehow we never seemed to come to any conclusions. I felt however, by the time that the three month period was over, that I had done what I could in seeking to reach out to them and had built up a genuine relationship with them. I just have to entrust them to the Lord, as I know only the Holy Spirit can convict them and save them.

I saw something of my sister too. She was

drinking quite heavily, and I was very concerned about her. She had not had a very easy life. Her husband was a schizophrenic and had been in and out of mental institutions or prisons for years, so she hardly ever saw him. I was sorry that she seemed to have such a bad deal in life as she was a likeable person. She worked as an audio-secretary and earned good money, but this certainly didn't buy her happiness.

All the family were glad that I was off drugs and they must have recognised that God had been responsible but I think they felt happier to give the credit for this to a person. Perhaps they thought that Tony was that person, although he always challenged them, insisting that it wasn't him but God who had delivered me.

I know that it can take a long time for some people to become Christians. In my own case there was a ten year period when God was working in my life, and I constantly pray that the same will happen for my family.

After I had returned to the country, opportunities began to arise for me to go to Youth Custody Centres with Tony. I was still very nervous about going out and speaking but, like Tony, I had a real burden for young people in trouble. I know that over 50 per cent of the young people in our penal institutions are there basically because of the sort of backgrounds they come from. I'm not making excuses for the things that they have done wrong but just stating a plain fact. Tony and I both believed that they all deserved a chance and needed to be shown that there was hope.

The first Youth Custody Centre I went to speak at was the place where Tony went every week, Portland. I could only go to the morning service because, at that time, ex-prisoners were not allowed into the institution itself and the chapel at Portland was situated outside the wall. Tony and other members of the team were able to go in during the afternoon to meet the thirty or so lads who had responded.

On sharing my testimony I began to realise that slowly but surely I was getting more confident in what I was doing. It is always hard to know what impact one is having upon the lives of those who are listening, but God has not asked us to live for results; He has only asked us to be faithful.

Another time Tony took me to Erlestoke Youth Custody centre and there I met Peter Saunt, a chaplain who is reaching out in the name of Jesus to many who are in his charge. I was quite surprised at the number of people who came to the service as these services were voluntary for the lads in Youth Custody Centres. As we were walking down the aisle I suddenly heard one lad say to another: 'Who's that old bird and that bald old geezer that's going to be speaking to us tonight?' That nearly put me off the whole thing, but in fact the evening went well. At the end we had a bit of a debate, where lads asked questions, and at least two boys who were in for drugs offences came up and spoke to me afterwards. A prison officer also made himself known to us and it was good to know that he was a brother in Christ.

Another Youth Custody centre I went to was Guy's Marsh. Again we were surprised at the number of young people who turned up for the service, as this again was voluntary. I felt that this went very well, as over one third of the lads in the institution appeared that evening and there was a very heated debate afterwards. Again, I had contact with a couple of lads who were in for drug offences. Perhaps the most interesting part of this meeting was that we had dinner with a Christian assistant governor and her husband before the actual service and it was good to be able to share Christ with people from such different backgrounds from mine and to know that we were one.

Perhaps one of the toughest places I ever went to was Pucklechurch Remand Centre. This was an institution for women and I found it more difficult to share with them openly about what had happened in my life than I did with young lads. However, God seemed to give me the words and people did seem to be listening, and many of the women there came up afterwards and asked for my address. Another interesting aspect of this meeting was that the governor of Pucklechurch was, in fact, working in Billwood Hall Borstal when I was there many years before, although we did not remember each other.

I really felt that God had called me to go back into institutions and to share what Christ had done for me. I feel strongly that these people need to hear that there is hope. So many are branded by society as being beyond hope, and yet God specialises in people who are apparently beyond hope and demonstrates His power by not only saving them from their sins, but transforming and renewing their lives. A scripture that has always meant a lot to me is Corinthians 1: 25–31, where it says God chooses the weak and foolish of the world to confound the strong and the wise. I know that if God did it for me, He can certainly do it for other people.

One thing I have learnt from my prison ministry is that people aren't going to fall down on their faces, immediately converted, but we must be faithful in our sowing and in time, as the Holy Spirit works in their lives, people will change.

A rather depressing side of working in prisons is seeing so many who make commitments and seem to go on with the Lord for a while, and then fall away. I have come to realise that the decision to go on with God is in three stages for people in prison. First there is the commitment that is made inside, then there is the recommitment when they get outside the gates, and then thirdly there is the time when temptation comes to them and they have to choose whether they will go back to the world or go on with God. I know from my own life, Tony's, Carole's and many others from similar backgrounds, that the real choice comes when the times of temptation have to be faced. I was saddened to meet so many people who seemed to be having such terrible problems many years after becoming Christians. It also saddened me to see those who had made commitments during previous sentences going back inside again. I don't condemn them and I know God doesn't condemn them, but I do wish that they could take advantage of all that God could offer them.

I also began to realise, through His work, the great need that there is for people not only to come to know Jesus, but also to know healing and deliverance in their lives, particularly healing of the emotions. I remember Tony talking to me once about Lazarus, who was resurrected by the living power of Jesus but was still bandaged up, and needed his friends to release him. I sometimes saw people who were trying to go on as Christians, but were walking as though they had a lump of lead around their ankles. Sometimes it wasn't their fault. Sometimes it was that other, more mature, Christians had failed to lead them into freedom, and not exercised the authority that they have in Jesus to release them from influences from the past, both satanic and emotional. I believe that the Church has to respond to the total need of people as they come to Christ.

I was now stepping out in what could be termed 'ministry', but I was very much aware of the need to have Tony or someone else like him alongside me, as I wasn't ready yet to minister on my own. But it was good to meet many individuals who are praying and caring for those in our penal institutions. I was glad to think that I could be a source of encouragement to them as they sought to reach out in a very difficult area of society. When I think of the fact that one third of the people in the penal institutions in this country are under twenty-one, I realise that there is a mammoth task ahead. I feel sure that God wants to use my testimony to bring hope to many in those institutions.

18: Abundant life

On a personal level my relationship with Jesus had changed a lot. I felt I was at last growing up as a Christian. I no longer had visions and the other manifestations of the Spirit that I used to have when I was a younger Christian. I am convinced that God allowed me to have these experiences to encourage me and to help me through a very difficult time. I had eventually, however, to learn to live by faith and not by sight.

I already saw that there could be a danger that meetings, especially high-powered charismatic meetings, could become almost like a fix to me. I had met Christians who seemed to live from one meeting to the next, and I certainly didn't want to be like that. I had the sense of Jesus being with me all the time, and quietly and confidently I began to feel that my relationship with Him was deepening. I suppose it's rather like a child growing up in a home. With the right guidance and discipline there comes a time when that child moves out into the world, secure and able to make its own way. I feel this is what Jesus wanted for me and that I was beginning to experience this for myself.

I had learnt a lot concerning ministering to other people. I had learnt to respond to the needs of those who were in want of salvation, deliverance, baptism in the Holy Spirit or emotional healing, and I had learnt to know when to call someone else in to pray alongside me. I knew this was very important, as it is so easy to get out of one's depth. I also learnt that there were certain people who it was just no use my talking to, and I would have to get someone else to do the talking.

This period was very positive for me as I was putting into action many things I had learnt in theory, and I was constantly learning new things. I sometimes became very aware of the spiritual warfare I was involved in, and was constantly aware of the pressures that one takes on oneself in seeking to help others. However, this was another wonderful thing that God had done for me. I was now able to cope with pressure: the daily pressures of everyday life, of meeting people with needs, of reaching out in the name of Jesus to a non-Christian world.

By now Carole and I were really becoming part of a team with Tony. I was glad to be working with him for I had seen that he was always trying to do so much, and it was good to know that I could now be a positive part of what he was doing. It was also great to see that we all had individual gifts and ministries, and these were slowly but surely developing. There had been a stage when I felt totally inadequate and useless, and yet God was beginning to show me more and more that I had specific gifts which could be used to His glory. Carole was also growing and developing and being used of God in a wonderful way.

About this time we began to get more and more frustrated with the number of negative programmes being shown on television, particularly dealing with the drugs problem. We felt there should be an alternative view offered. We had begun to recognise that our combined testimonies were very powerful and we began to want to do something about what was going on in society. Television and the other media always put over the negative stories of drug addiction, and so few people were showing the positive side: that many, many addicts are now totally free and living fulfilled lives in society through the power of Jesus. Thinking about this, we felt that perhaps we should resurrect the 'Life' presentations that we had done the previous year. Eventually we decided that we should together reach out in the name of Jesus, using an adaptation of the old 'Life' presentation, to endeavour to be a witness in various areas, in the local churches, prisons and schools, of what Jesus could do.

We were already used to ministering together and through living close together we had many opportunities of praying and sharing and being involved together in various activities. However, this was going to be different. We were all quite excited at the different ideas that were coming into our minds at that time. Tony was certainly the focal point of all that was happening, but we in our spirits witnessed that this was right. We started to plan two different projects. The first was really to get the coffee bar going, to be used as a base both for Tony's Prison Christian Fellowship work and any work that I would do with him in this line, and also as a base for our second project: to reach out nationally to people on drugs with the message of hope.

Almost miraculously, Tony acquired a building for the coffee bar in a nearby seaside town. He had written to the YMCA movement and asked them if he could use their building. Only a month previously the regional executive had met to discuss this building and had shelved the decision concerning its sale, but receiving Tony's letter they decided that they would let him have the building. Within weeks Tony had installed his office there and we had started to go down to help clearing it up and decorating it, as it was very run down. Within a couple of months we were ready for the dedication.

It was wonderful to see the number of people who turned up for this dedication: over fifty people, from the YMCA movement, from the local churches, and friends of ours who came just to pray with us on that evening and commit the building to the Lord. As with any new situation there was a time of chaos, but gradually that chaos sorted out into some kind of order. First of all God supplied over £4,000, which was a real miracle, and enabled us to do all the rewiring and basic decoration and structural work which needed doing to make the building safe. But most important of all, we found that there were many older Christians who were really committed to praying for us and supporting us in any work we were to do.

It had been arranged that the coffee bar should open on the day of a national Folk Festival which was to take place in the town, and suddenly we were in at the deep end. Crowds of children turned up and we felt as though we were quite overrun with them. We had a team down to help us from the Newbury YMCA. They were a group of young and older Christians who were hoping to get a coffee bar started up there. As the first week progressed various people came to the coffee bar. It was a very low key type of evangelism, as we merely befriended and got to know individuals, but occasionally there was an opportunity to talk about the Lord.

After a while, Tony decided that we should go out

and hold open air meetings in the evenings for a week and this we started to do. The first night, a bit like the first presentations that we did, didn't go very well, but eventually we found that we were getting more and more confident and I found I was able to speak sometimes twice in an evening, sharing with the many people who strolled past on the promenade, looking down at us on the beach. Commitments were made that week and I know the gospel of Jesus was proclaimed in a very open way. I could never have imagined that I would have been able to speak in the open air like this, and yet there I was speaking out for Jesus. I had learnt a long time ago that even if one has a headache or feels sick inside with tension, if one steps out in faith, then God honours that. This happened for me every night. Carole joined me at the microphone each night, and many others shared, while Tony basically linked the meeting together.

We are still very young in our work in this coffee bar, but already I am finding that there are individual children and older people with whom I am developing relationships, which are based on Jesus. I firmly believe that as we keep this place open, Jesus will send the people whom He knows we can help.

We have also been busy with the 'Life' presentations, and are all set to go on at least one or two mini-tours over the next six to nine months. We are already preparing to go to up north where we will be reaching out in a large Pentecostal church, speaking to the local Lydia and other intercessory groups, going into two prisons, and a local Youth Custody Centre. More and more people are asking us to go and share.

There was a time when I felt I should try to hide some of the unacceptable aspects of my past, and I know there is always a danger that testimonies can be misused or abused, but now I know what I want to do with my testimony. I want it to be brought to people who have given up hope. As I think about all the different things I am involved with now and all the different hopes and future commitments I have made I can only say that I know what it is to have abundant life, as Jesus promised. I have the blessing of knowing that all things are working together for good, because Jesus is in control of my life.

As I reflect on all that has happened to me and all that is happening to me now I can only, from the deepest part of my heart, thank Jesus for everything that He has done. I hope that Christian readers have been encouraged by hearing what God has done for me. And for those who do not know Him, my dearest hope is that you will turn to the one who loves you far more abundantly than anyone else could ever love you – The Lord Jesus.

Both Anita and Tony would be pleased to hear from readers who have been moved or challenged by Anita's story.
They can be contacted at:

YMCA,
Mill Street,
Sidmouth,
Devon,
England.

ESCAPE TO REALITY

Michael Tony Ralls with David Hall

Psychiatrists described him as an incurable addict beyond help; official reports labelled him as a compulsive criminal. After spending seven years between the ages of 16 and 25 in various institutions, a pawn in a bureaucratic game, it is small wonder that society had given up on Tony. But he wasn't beyond the reach of the love of God, who gently transformed his life from destruction.

'Nothing is down to me. It's Jesus who has done it.' That's the testimony he now shares as he works alongside many addicts and prisoners who suffer a similar plight.

A New Wine Paperback
£2.50

THE BITTER HARVEST

Michael Tony Ralls

This analysis of the 1960's age of permissiveness and the Swinging Sixties shows how as a society we are now reaping the bitter harvest of what we sowed then, with the seeds sown then now producing their fruit of lawlessness, violence, broken homes, divorce and all manner of social problems.

Children born at that time are now adults and have had virtually no biblical or moral standards taught to them. It is therefore no wonder that we see rising crime, rising divorce and social unrest with no solution other than turning to the saving power of the gospel of Christ.

A New Wine Paperback
£2.50
Also available on cassette
The Bitter Harvest Songs
£4.95

LIFE

MICHAEL TONY RALLS

an album of songs by

Michael Tony Ralls

Tony is a Regional Co-ordinator with Prison Christian Fellowship – an organisation undertaking Christian work among Prisoners and Prison Staff. As an ex-prisoner himself he is all too aware of the needs found in Prison life. The songs contained on this album stem from Tony's experience and cover a range of styles.

The recording of **'Life'** has been approached in the same way as one might approach the writing of an autobiography. Tony has not attempted to emulate professional Gospel artistes but rather to express the life of Christ that is in him through the medium of music. This fresh approach to recording has given this album an appeal and ability to minister that will probably outlast many more 'highly polished' Christian records on the market today.

Tony's desire in recording **'Life'** is that his songs, along with the written testimony on the sleeve should get into the hands of those who can relate to his experience – those who unfortunately the Church often fails to reach. Whether you buy a copy for yourself, a friend in need or for your local prison, we believe that this album has a lot to offer.

'Life' is available on both album and cassette. Copies may be obtained through your local Christian Bookshop. All profits from sales will go to Prison Christian Fellowship and other trusts working in the same field.